Nuggets from
God
and Mom

Nuggets from
God
and Mom

Margaret Henson King

Call to me and I will answer you and tell you great and
unsearchable things you do not know.
Jeremiah 33:3

WESTBOW
P R E S S
A DIVISION OF THOMAS NELSON

WestBow Press books may be ordered through booksellers or by contacting:

WestBow Press
A Division of Thomas Nelson
1663 Liberty Drive
Bloomington, IN 47403
www.westbowpress.com
1-(866) 928-1240

Because of the dynamic nature of the Internet, any Web addresses or links contained in this book may have changed since publication and may no longer be valid. The views expressed in this work are solely those of the author and do not necessarily reflect the views of the publisher, and the publisher hereby disclaims any responsibility for them.

ISBN: 978-1-4497-0641-8 (sc)
ISBN: 978-1-4497-0642-5 (e)

Library of Congress Control Number: 2010938168

Printed in the United States of America
WestBow Press rev. date: 10/25/2010

Dedication

To Joe,

who has enriched my life through his

unfailing support, encouragement, and love.

Mark 4:33,34

With many similar parables Jesus spoke the word to them, as much as they could understand. He did not say anything to them without using a parable. But when He was alone with His own disciples, He explained everything.

Most of the time, even those closest to Jesus did not fully understand what He meant when He spoke to the crowds. Yet, when He was alone with the disciples, He explained everything. Sometimes we don't understand either. We can read and hear the Word of God, and though it might make sense, it just doesn't soak into our hearts. We don't really get it. When we spend time alone with Him, He makes the meaning of His words clearer. The truths contained in the Scripture can soak in and become a part of us. In Jeremiah 33:3, God says, "Call to me and I will answer you and tell you great and unsearchable things you do not know." There are thousands of golden nuggets hiding away in the Word of God. Spend some time alone with Him today and let Him explain them to you.

Romans 12:1b (The Message)

Take your everyday, ordinary life—your sleeping, eating, going-to-work, and walking-around life—and place it before God as an offering.

Many people think they have nothing to offer God. All that God really wants from us requires no special talent, no great intelligence, no enormous wealth, no important position, and no political power. He wants us. Our highest calling is to bring Him pleasure. What pleases Him? It is our devotion, our company, and our love. We can't put Him in a box somewhere, attempting to honor Him on Sunday morning only and occasionally through the week. He wants to be our constant companion, acknowledged as the vital part of our life that He is. There is an offering you can bring Him more precious than all the gold and diamonds in the world. It is you, just as you are.

2 Thessalonians 3:3

But the Lord is faithful, and He will strengthen and protect you from the evil one.

As a child of God, I sometimes wish I were just a baby in His arms or at least a toddler on His knee. I would prefer to live a life without trouble or temptation of any kind…but that's what we can expect in Heaven, not here. We will have trials of all kinds, and our battles are real. However, God has promised us strength and protection from Satan's attacks on our lives, and we will always be victorious if we lean on Him. We may be wounded, and we may be exhausted; but God calls us to crawl back up on His lap and rest in the shadow of His wings. "Come unto me," He says, "and I will give you rest." What a wonderful God we serve!

1 Corinthians 13:5b

(Love) is not easily angered, it keeps no record of wrongs.

Satan has many tools to use against us, tempting us to act in ways unbecoming to Christians. One of the ways he tempts us is through convincing us that we have a right to be angry with others. People--even people who care about us--will do things to upset and hurt us. Sometimes they even do it intentionally. We can remember the 'injustice' forever if we choose. We can let our feelings seethe away, and we can let our grudges consume us. We can choose to sin by getting even when God Himself has told us that vengeance is His. Or…we can follow Jesus' example. He asked God to forgive the men who mocked

Him, spat upon Him, beat Him, and nailed Him to a cross. If we want to live our lives for Him, then we must let His love show through us by being slow to anger and forgiving to those who hurt us. I pray that you will be able to tear up your mental list of wrongs against you and let the love of Christ fill every corner of your mind and heart.

Exodus 3:7,8a

The Lord said, "I have indeed seen the misery of my people in Egypt. I have heard them crying out because of their slave drivers, and I am concerned about their suffering. So I have come down to rescue them."

There is only one solution to every seemingly impossible problem we will ever have. It is God. Friends and family can be a source of great comfort, but God has the answers. He knows every single thing that causes us grief, misery, pain, or fear; and He is willing to rescue us. As long as we think we can find solutions ourselves, He will allow us to flounder around to search for them. However, recognizing our total dependence upon Him will move His hands. Our complete rescue comes only when we acknowledge His power and cry out to the Only One who can save us.

Psalm 36:7,8

How priceless is your unfailing love! Both high and low among men find refuge in the shadow of your wings. They feast on the abundance of your house; you give them drink from your river of delights.

The world has a way of assigning more importance to one person than another. Others may consider money, looks, talents, ability, position, or something else. The truth is, we are equal in God's eyes. Each of us can feast on the abundance of His house and drink from His river of delights if we will just abide in Him. How wonderful! Notice, though, that these blessings aren't promised to us when we are out in the briars and thistles checking out what the world has to offer. They come when we stay in the shadow of His wings. Feasting on the abundance of God's house is far more than having food: it is having every need met. Drinking from His river of delights is joy reserved for God's children who are living in obedience. He adores us, and He has great rewards even in this life for those who live their lives close to Him.

James 3:17,18

But the wisdom that comes from heaven is first of all pure; then peace-loving, considerate, submissive, full of mercy and good fruit, impartial and sincere. Peacemakers who sow in peace raise a harvest of righteousness.

Wisdom from God begins with living a holy life. We cannot expect God to give us revelation in complicated situations when we are not willing to follow the specific instructions He has already given us. Being obedient is a prerequisite to gaining wisdom. The evidence of wisdom from God is apparent in the way we treat others. We must be gentle, reasonable, merciful, sincere, and impartial…and we must be peacemakers. Yes, it takes effort, but it is not impossible. Opportunities will present themselves if we are looking. Make every effort to treat others as God wants, and strive to bring peace wherever, whenever you can.

Acts 4:13

When they saw the courage of Peter and John and realized that they were unschooled, ordinary men, they were astonished and they took note that these men had been with Jesus.

Jesus made an astonishing difference in the lives of Peter and John. They spoke with courage and boldness, and even though they were uneducated, ordinary men, they had a great impact on those who heard them. They were faithful, open, and willing to be used. As a result, they were great witnesses for the Lord and won many souls to Him. Jesus has made an astonishing difference in our lives, too. He has blessed us in countless ways, taken away all our sins, and given us each of us a new heart. The education we have had doesn't really make a difference, nor do the talents He has given us. All of us who love Him can honor Him by being faithful, open, and willing to be used...and living our lives so people can see that we have been with Jesus.

John 5:7,8

"Sir," the invalid replied, "I have no one to help me into the pool when the water is stirred. While I am trying to get in, someone else goes down ahead of me." Then Jesus said to him, "Get up! Pick up your mat and walk."

In the passage before this, Jesus had asked the lame man if he wanted to be made whole. The invalid replied with excuses: no one would help him, and others got in his way. Jesus answered by telling him to get up and do something himself. Do not think I am suggesting that a person with a handicap can just decide to be well, but this principle does apply to us in many areas of our lives. Few of us could say that we have never been hurt or hampered by someone else's actions, and we could spend our lives blaming those people for our problems. But blaming others, no matter how much they may be at fault, doesn't solve a thing. Our happiness, our wholeness, and our victory lie in our relationship with Jesus and our obedience to Him. If anything is causing you to be less than you can be, do as your Lord and King says. Look to Him as your only source and rely on Him to give you strength. Then pick up your mat and walk.

Hebrews 10:16,17

"This is the covenant I will make with them after that time," says the Lord. "I will put my laws in their hearts, and I will write them on their minds." Then He adds: "Their sins and lawless acts I will remember no more."

The Eternal God, Ruler of the Universe, has made a binding, solemn promise concerning those who accept Him as Lord and King. We don't have to depend upon a human high priest to read us the law and offer sacrifices to atone for our sins as the Hebrews did. We are not down here on earth floundering around hopelessly trapped in the muck of sin and not knowing how to escape. God Himself writes His laws on our minds and puts them in our hearts. And--when we fail, Jesus, the perfect Lamb of God, has already sacrificed Himself to pay for our redemption. Our sins are gone. God has forgotten them. What a loving, merciful Father! Let these amazing promises overshadow anything that may be wrong in your life today.

Judges 6:14

The Lord turned to him (Gideon) and said, "Go in the strength you have and save Israel out of Midian's hand. Am I not sending you?"

God had a job for Gideon. Gideon had no special talent or training, no time for months and years of preparations. In the whole scheme of things, some people might have thought him to be a "nobody." In addition, God could have wiped the Midianites off the face of the earth with a word, but He chose to use a man. "Go in your own strength," God told him. In other words, "Don't wait for some miraculous power to come to you. Just trust me." I wonder how many times we have missed something miraculous because we were not willing to do just that--trust. The truth is, if God wants us to do something, we can. We may shake and quake in our sandals at the thought, but when it comes time for us to step out, God's strength will lift us up and give us all the power we need. God has a job for you. He probably isn't asking you to save your country, but whatever He does ask, He will give you what you need to accomplish it. Don't ignore Him when you feel His nudge and hear Him speaking to your heart. "Am I not sending you?" When God asks, that's all you need.

Matthew 9:18

While He was saying this, a ruler came and knelt before Him and said, "My daughter has just died. But come and put your hand on her, and she will live."

The ruler's daughter had just died. Her life was over, or so it seemed. This father, though a ruler himself, could do nothing--nothing, that is, except reach out to Jesus. Jesus touched her, and her life was restored. The event recounted here is a great miracle, no doubt. It is no greater, though, than His touch upon daughters and sons today...the touch that heals us from the brokenness of spiritual death. The hands of Jesus in our lives can restore us no matter how far we may have wandered. He can give us back our hope, our joy, and our peace. His touch is the only thing that gives us life worth living. I pray His hand is mighty upon you today.

Habakkuk 3:17,18

Though the fig tree does not bud and there are no grapes on the vines, though the olive crop fails and the fields produce no food, though there are no sheep in the pen and no cattle in the stalls, yet I will rejoice in the LORD, I will be joyful in God my Savior.

In my mind, I can imagine Habakkuk standing tall, chin up, shoulders back. He was determined that even though his world might be falling apart around him, he would still rejoice. It is a fact that we all face trouble, disappointment, loss, and challenges of all kinds. We feel weak, and we feel helpless. We hurt, and we fail. No matter what our circumstances, God is with us…and He is in control. He is working in our lives to cause all things to work together for our good--all things--even the heart-breaking, gut-wrenching, nightmarish ones. He is our strength, and He will not fail us. Trust Him. Rejoice and be glad.

Isaiah 65:24

Before they call I will answer; while they are still speaking I will hear.

In this passage, God is speaking of His chosen people, including us. We are a part of His family because we have accepted His free gift of salvation through Jesus Christ. There is a reason you are reading this: God is reminding you how much He wants to bless your life. Have you ever stopped to think how many wonderful things He has done for you that you didn't ask Him to do? How many times has He rescued you when you didn't even know you were in danger? You don't really have to tell God what you need; He knows it before you do. Prayer is acknowledging that He is the Giver of all good things, Creator, Lord, and Master. It is spending intimate time with the One who loves you more than anyone here on earth ever could. It is staying close to the One who gave you life and sustains you day-by-day, hour-by-hour, and minute-by-minute. Visit with God today. Don't wait until you need something. Spend time with Him because He loves you.

Ephesians 3:20,21

Now to Him who is able to do immeasurably more than all we ask or imagine, according to His power that is at work within us, to Him be glory in the church and in Christ Jesus throughout all generations, forever and ever! Amen.

Do you ever consider that you may be settling for less in life than God has for you? He wants us to have abundant life; in fact, Christ Himself stated that was one of the reasons He came to earth (John 10:10). We serve a God who is able and willing to give us more than enough--more than enough strength, more than enough wisdom, more than enough joy. There is no limit and no end to His power, and this power is at work within us! Whatever your mind can imagine, God can do more...and you can be more when you are yielded to His will. Don't limit Him by thinking too small or expecting too little. We serve a great God.

Isaiah 46:3

Listen to me, O house of Jacob, all you who remain of the house of Israel, you whom I have upheld since you were conceived, and have carried since your birth.

How long has God been involved in our lives? He told Jeremiah that He knew him before He formed him in the womb. This verse tells us that He has upheld us since we were conceived and carried us since our birth. He loved us and made plans for our lives from the beginning of time. He decided where and when we would be born; He put others in our lives to give us direction, comfort, joy, and love. Greatest of all, He sent Jesus, who gave His life to pay for our sins. I can't begin to explain how much He loves you, but He can. Spend some quiet time with Him today and let Him remind you again how much He loves you.

Deuteronomy 7:9

Know therefore that the Lord your God is God; He is the faithful God, keeping His covenant of love to a thousand generations of those who love Him and keep His commands.

We should thank God every day if we were blessed with godly ancestors. I have no doubt that I escaped deadly snares because of my ancestors' faithfulness to Him. But even if you weren't so blessed, your descendants can be. When we commit ourselves to God and do our best to follow His commands, we don't have a life of peace and joy for ourselves only; we also leave a priceless legacy to our descendants for a thousand generations! God has promised to keep His covenant of love to them as well as to us. There are millions of reasons to be a child of God; some of them are the blessings our children, grandchildren, great-grandchildren (on and on) will receive because of God's promises to us. That inheritance beats any inheritance of money, houses, or land we could leave them.

Luke 15:23,24

"Bring the fatted calf and kill it. Let's have a feast and celebrate. For this son of mine was dead and is alive gain; he was lost and is found." So they began to celebrate.

The parable of the prodigal son is a wonderful example of God's love. Though the son had been blessed, part of his father's family, he willingly left to become a part of the world. When he got to the point that he was wallowing and eating with the pigs, he went back to his father, hoping only for crumbs. His father joyfully ran to meet him, put the best robes on him, and ordered a feast. Like the prodigal son, we can't mess up so much that God won't welcome us back with open arms. He will clean off the stench of our sins and order a celebration. He loves us that much, and He will always love us, plain and simple. Whether we have just a toe in the wallowing hole or have fallen headlong, today is the perfect day to go back home.

Judges 6:12

When the angel of the Lord appeared to Gideon, he said, "The Lord is with you, mighty warrior."

At the time the angel spoke, Gideon was threshing wheat inside a winepress, hiding from the Midianites. According to Gideon's own words in verse 15, he was the least member of the weakest clan in Manasseh. In his own eyes, he was anything but a warrior; but God saw him differently. God wanted Gideon to perform no small task (destroying the enemy of the Israelites), and He gave him the strength, courage, and ability to accomplish it. God could use Gideon to rescue the Israelites because Gideon was willing. God has tasks for each of us, too. It's doubtful He will send an angel to tell us, but He will lay it on our hearts…and once we have submitted to His will, He will give us the strength, courage, and ability to accomplish what He has asked. We are God's warriors. We must be willing to battle whatever forces invade our lives and the lives of those around us. Put on your armor and fight the enemy today. Be a mighty warrior.

Psalm 32:8,9

I will instruct you and teach you in the way you should go; I will counsel you and watch over you. Do not be like the horse or the mule, which have no understanding but must be controlled by bit and bridle or they will not come to you.

We were not created and then abandoned to face life on our own. Our creator had a plan for us when He laid the foundation of the world, and He has been gently leading us since we were born. Look at the things He does: He instructs us, teaches us, counsels us, and watches over us. In other Scriptures, He encourages us to learn of Him and to write His words on our hearts. Still, He allows us to choose, to decide on our own whether we obey or not. He exerts no power or force even though He is the Almighty, All-powerful One. I have sometimes wished that God did have a bridle on me. It would have saved me much heartache if He had forced me to stay on the path He has laid out for me. But, that's not our God. He wants our obedience to come because of our love for Him, and He gently, patiently leads us day by day, moment by moment, to see us safely home.

2 Corinthians 5:7

We live by faith, not by sight.

I am a native of Missouri, the Show-Me State. We Missourians are known for needing proof before we believe, but this is a human trait shared by many. As much as any of us would like to know and understand everything, we please God when we just trust Him. He wants us to accept His Word without doubt and His will without question. Our faith pleases Him, and it is what sustains us through the struggles of this life. I truly believe that the amount of joy and peace we experience here on earth depends upon our willingness to trust Him with everything, especially when we don't see or understand. God has promised to protect us, defend us, provide for us, and love us forever. Jesus gave His life to redeem us. Who could need more proof than that?

John 15:1,2

I am the true vine, and my Father is the gardener. He cuts off every branch in me that bears no fruit, while every branch that does bear fruit He prunes so that it will be even more fruitful.

I understand the concept of pruning vines and trees, but I still cringe just a little when I see it done. I doubt that the branches, if they could think, would believe it was best for them. Yet we know that these branches become stronger and bear more fruit when they are pruned. It's the same for us. We don't want to be pruned, but it will happen nonetheless, probably when we least expect it. It happens to every branch in Christ that bears no fruit and every branch that does. It is a painful process, but when the wounds heal, we are stronger. Sometimes we are able to see the reasons for the pruning; sometimes we can't. The fact remains that our heavenly Father knows what things are keeping us from producing the best fruit we can for His Kingdom; because He loves us, He works in our lives to help us make changes. Trust Him even when you are hurting, and believe that you will be stronger and more productive because of your trials.

Ephesians 2:10

For we are God's workmanship, created in Christ Jesus to do good works, which God prepared in advance for us to do.

God created us and saved us to do good works. He even prepared these works in advance. Some people have the attitude that they are doing God a favor if they help someone else, but that's not the case. He doesn't need us to do it. After all, He can speak, and it will be accomplished. He can comfort, care for, encourage, and lift up each person all on His own, without our help. He has given us tasks to do for our own benefit, and when we do the works God has prepared for us to do, we are helping ourselves. We are increasing our joy, building our faith, growing in our love, and deepening our relationship with the Creator of everything. Do yourself a favor today. Help someone else.

Luke 5:4, 5

When He (Jesus) had finished speaking, He said to Simon, "Put out into deep water, and let down the nets for a catch."

Simon answered, "Master, we've worked hard all night and haven't caught anything. But because you say so, I will let down the nets."

Simon Peter was a fisherman by profession. Jesus, in the eyes of those around Him, was just a carpenter's son. The idea that Jesus would know more about where and when to fish seemed ridiculous to human reasoning. His instructions just didn't make any sense. Peter could have said, "I know what I am doing. Just let me do things my way. Besides, I have done all I want to do and am too tired to do any more." But

Peter recognized the authority of Jesus and said (in his own way), "My mind doesn't understand why you want me to do this, deep down I don't really want to, and it won't be easy for me to do. BUT, because you tell me to, I will do it." There are times when the Lord may ask us to do something that is hard for us--something that we don't want to do--something that our human reasoning (or Satan) speaks against. Then we need to trust enough to say, "Even though I don't want to do this thing and I don't understand why I should, because you say so, I will do it." He always knows what's best for us, and obeying Him is the only path to peace and happiness.

1 Samuel 3:10

The Lord came and stood there, calling as at the other times, "Samuel! Samuel!" Then Samuel said, "Speak, Lord, for your servant is listening."

It is doubtful that any of us will ever physically hear the voice of the Lord calling to us this side of Heaven. However, He can and does speak to us in other ways every day. He speaks to us through others if we are open; He speaks to us through His Word if we will read it; and He speaks to our hearts if we will seek Him. Samuel's response to God's calling is so simple, yet so complete. Like Samuel, we should all say, "I am your servant, Lord, and I am listening to your voice. Tell me what you want." God has a plan for each of us that will bring us more joy than we can imagine. Listen for His voice, guiding you, consoling you, encouraging you, strengthening you, lifting you up, telling you of His forgiveness, and reminding you how much He loves you. Hear Him. Then use His words to shape your life.

Romans 8:18

I consider that our present sufferings are not worth comparing with the glory that will be revealed in us.

We all have trouble on this earth. No one who has ever lived has had smooth sailing throughout life. Satan's plan is for us to sink in waters of self-pity, self-doubt, bitterness, and remorse, drowning our hope. But God's children have another option. We can climb in Jesus' arms and let Him carry us safely to the other side of the stormy sea. Paul says that however much we may be suffering in the present, it doesn't compare to the glory (praise, honor, extreme joy), which will be revealed in us. Whatever storm you're in today, remind yourself that it is temporary. Almighty God loves you, and there is a glorious tomorrow for you, Child of the King!

1 Thessalonians 3:9

How can we thank God enough for you in return for all the joy we have in the presence of our God because of you?

One of the greatest joys in this life is to see those we care about living their lives devoted to God. This should be our greatest hope for them… more than wealth, position, fame, or power. This is because we know that only through yielding our lives to God can we have peace, joy, and eternal security. Every day we should thank God for calling out to those we love, speaking to their hearts and granting them forgiveness and eternal salvation. Even if your loved ones seem far away from Him, thank God for His plan you cannot see, working in their lives to draw them back. Then allow the joy, which comes only through trusting Him, to fill your day and your heart.

Acts 20:32

Now I commit you to God and to the word of His grace, which can build you up and give you an inheritance among all those who are sanctified.

Paul was saying goodbye to the Ephesians, whom He had been teaching for three years. He had done what he could, and he now trusted their future to God. He knew that God's grace was sufficient. This is a lesson that some of us have trouble getting: sometimes we should move on, too. I'm not talking about turning our backs on family or friends; I am talking about truly giving a circumstance, problem, or person to God and letting Him do a wondrous work. We should be willing to help others when we can, but we do not have all the answers. God does. He is the source of all happiness, all health, all wealth, all love, all hope, and all joy. He's perfectly able to run the Universe. Give Him your cares and enjoy the blessings He has given you.

Isaiah 41:9,10

I took you from the ends of the earth; from its farthest corners I called you. I said, "You are my servant;" I have chosen you and not rejected you. So do not fear, for I am with you; do not be dismayed, for I am your God. I will strengthen you and help you; I will uphold you with my righteous right hand."

If God was not reaching out to you, you wouldn't be reading this passage of Scripture. God chose you. You. It says in Psalms that He knew each of us before He formed us and before He laid the foundations of the world. He didn't put us here on earth and then leave us to struggle, facing trial after trial on our own. He is with us always, telling us not to be afraid or dismayed. He acknowledges us as His children, promising to strengthen, help, and uphold us. How much heartache and worry would we save ourselves if we lived as though we believed these promises? Don't be afraid or dismayed. You are in the hands of your God, the All-Powerful Creator of the Universe.

John 1:45,46 (The Message)

Philip went and found Nathanael and told him, "We've found the One Moses wrote of in the Law, the One preached by the prophets. It's Jesus, Joseph's son, the one from Nazareth!" Nathanael said, "Nazareth? You've got to be kidding." But Philip said, "Come and see for yourself."

Nathanael could have missed the greatest opportunity of his life. He could have been too busy, too skeptical, too apathetic, or too burdened down with guilt to go meet Jesus. As it was, he took the steps needed to meet Jesus in person, and it changed his life for all eternity. Knowing and loving Jesus doesn't require great effort or great sacrifice. It doesn't require great knowledge or a series of complicated rituals. Best of all, it doesn't require an unspotted, guilt-free life. All it takes is the desire to meet Him face to face, allowing His love and peace to permeate our hearts. No experience we can ever have upon this earth compares with a loving relationship with Christ. I pray that you already know this; if not, come and see for yourself.

2 Corinthians 4:6

For God, who said, "Let light shine out of darkness," made His light shine in our hearts to give us the light of the knowledge of the glory of God in the face of Christ.

This is a mind-boggling thought. God, who created the sun, moon, and all the stars in the Universe, cared enough about us to make His light shine in our hearts! We are not doomed to live in darkness--deceived, confused, and oblivious to the truth that Christ came to rescue us from this darkness. Because of this light, we can know beyond a doubt that Christ lives today. He is at the right hand of God, and His Spirit lives in our hearts, encouraging and helping us. I pray that the light that God has placed within you will always illuminate your path, warm your heart, and spill out to others along your way.

James 3:7,8

All kinds of animals, birds, reptiles, and creatures of the sea are being tamed and have been tamed by man, but no man can tame the tongue. It is a restless evil, full of deadly poison.

The prospect of taming the tongue sounds hopeless, doesn't it? The Bible is full of warnings if we aren't careful what we say and promises of blessings if we are, yet James says no man can tame the tongue. No man can, but God can. If we are willing to listen to the Spirit within us, to weigh our words before speaking, we can control what we say. How many times have we heard people say, "I probably shouldn't say this, but...." When they are finished, someone else has been embarrassed, shamed, criticized, slandered, or demeaned in some other way. Something deep inside them warned them not to speak, but they did it anyway. If we want to please God, we must listen for His leading in whatever we do and whatever we say. If you feel the need to begin a sentence with, "I probably shouldn't say this," then don't say it.

1 Samuel 24:12

May the Lord judge between you and me. And may the Lord avenge the wrongs you have done to me, but my hand will not touch you.

Saul had schemed against David and plotted to kill him. David had to flee for his life. However, when he had a chance to kill Saul, he did not. He was willing to let God be the judge and punish Saul for the wrong he had done. I hope we will never have someone plotting to kill us, but there are countless other ways that people intentionally hurt each other. The trouble others may bring upon us, though, pales in comparison to the problems we can cause ourselves when we set out to get even. Seeking revenge fills our lives with turmoil and robs us of our joy and peace. Even the time spent in remembering and reliving offenses against us is wasted time. No matter how badly we have been hurt, we can spoil Satan's plans to destroy us if we leave revenge to God. He is a fair and righteous judge, for only He really knows the motives and the hearts of others. What blessed relief we can have when we can say as David did: "May the Lord avenge the wrongs you have done to me, but my hand will not touch you."

Jeremiah 32:17

Ah, Sovereign Lord, you have made the heavens and the earth by your great power and outstretched arm. Nothing is too hard for you.

I can imagine Jeremiah nodding his head and saying, "Ah...I get it." He recognized the awesome power that created the heavens, earth, and everything in them. He realized that God didn't even have to work up a sweat to create it all. He did it with an outstretched arm (and a few words). If God could do all that, He can do anything. There is such comfort in this truth. Life may seem too hard for us sometimes, but it isn't hard for God. No matter what anyone says or thinks about the circumstances of our lives, we are God's children. Our loving Heavenly Father can heal what's hurting, fix what's broken, and make everything all better. He holds our hands when things are hard, and He carries us when we can't walk. We can always face the future with hope because Almighty God has our future in His hands. Nothing is too hard for Him…and besides that, He adores us! Do you get it?

2 Corinthians 10:3-5

For though we live in the world, we do not wage war as the world does. The weapons we fight with are not the weapons of the world. On the contrary, they have divine power to demolish strongholds. We demolish arguments and every pretension that sets itself up against the knowledge of God, and we take captive every thought to make it obedient to Christ.

We do have a mighty enemy, but God is almighty. He has given us the weapons we need to wage war, and these weapons have divine power! Isn't that amazing? Our weapons have the power to defeat the plots and schemes Satan brings against us…and not just defeat them, either. We can totally demolish strongholds, things that cause us to fear or try to take God's place in our lives. Satan tries to mess with our minds so much, but we don't have to be bogged down with wrong thinking. It is possible to make our thoughts obedient to Christ. Do you know what the strongholds in your mind are? Wage war against them. Get your sword with divine power and demolish them. The Bible tells us Satan will flee if we resist him. Speak God's Word and drive him off. Spend your day as God intended, filled with His peace.

2 Timothy 1:12b

Yet I am not ashamed, because I know whom I have believed, and am convinced that He is able to guard what I have entrusted to Him for that day.

My favorite words in this Scripture are "(I) am convinced that He is able." Paul knew Jesus; therefore, he knew beyond a shadow of a doubt that Jesus is able. Notice the end of the verse, though: Christ is able to guard or keep what we give to Him. Being totally convinced in our minds that Jesus can take care of any problem is one thing. Letting Him take care of the problem is another thing. How much peace have we lost because we don't wait for God and allow Him to take care of our problems in His time and in His way? We have to commit our cares to Him and be willing to wait for Him to work His plan in our lives, trusting that He is able. If we can't do that, are we really convinced? Are you convinced in your heart that He is able? Then let go of your problems and give them to Him.

Psalm 32:3-5

When I kept silent, my bones wasted away through my groaning all day long. For day and night your hand was heavy upon me; my strength was sapped as in the heat of summer. Then I acknowledged my sin to you and did not cover up my iniquity. I said, "I will confess my transgressions to the Lord"—and you forgave the guilt of my sin.

No one has ever lived who has not sinned except Jesus Himself. Most of us have been caught up in something that we knew was wrong, but we preferred to ignore the truth. Without a doubt, there were undesirable consequences. That's because God loves us too much to leave us trapped in the muck and mire of sin. He constantly calls to us, and if we are too stubborn to listen, things will just get uglier and uglier until we do. Do you believe that? David experienced it. Just look at how sin was weighing him down. But (here's the hallelujah part) he acknowledged his sin to God, and God forgave him. How simple is that? Receiving

God's forgiveness is not difficult. We need to confess our sin to God, stop it, and accept the gift Jesus made possible. What a deal!

Jeremiah 6:16a

This is what the Lord says: "Stand at the crossroads and look; ask for the ancient paths, ask where the good way is, and walk in it, and you will find rest for your souls."

We have decisions to make every day. Some we know are important; some may not seem significant at the time but may affect our lives drastically down the road. God warns us that for every crossroad we encounter and every decision we make, we must seek to choose the way He wants us to go. Notice that He doesn't expect us to make decisions hastily. We are supposed to stand and look, considering the consequences for taking whatever path we choose. We are supposed to ask God, waiting for answers. Then when we choose the good way, the way He established long ago, we will find rest for our souls. If you are at a crossroads in your life, don't make a move without seeking God. Ask Him where the good way is and walk in it. Then expect Him to be with you every step, filling your life with peace and rest.

Proverbs 4:18

The path of the righteous is like the first gleam of dawn, shining ever brighter till the full light of day.

Having lived my early years as an adventurous tomboy, I can tell you a thing or two about paths. If you don't know where they lead, you may end up somewhere you don't want to be. When you can't see where you are headed, you are, sooner or later, going to stumble and fall, get attacked by a varmint, slide down some dangerous slope, or get turned around and lost. In some areas, you could even find yourself in quicksand. The path through life is filled with pitfalls, too, but we don't have to hack our way through the brush to find a safe way. When we accepted Christ as our Savior, we were clothed in His righteousness, and it is this righteousness that shines on our path through life, showing us the way. The farther we travel with Him, the more clearly we can see and the easier our journey becomes. We don't have to live in the thicket of confusion and uncertainty; Christ has shown us the way.

Philemon 1:7

Your love has given me great joy and encouragement, because you, brother, have refreshed the hearts of the saints.

There are many Scriptures that make it clear that Jesus wants us to love one another. He wants us to have an unselfish, loyal concern for their good. We need to care, and we need to show it. How does our love affect others? It brings joy and encouragement, and it refreshes their hearts! Think about that last one. Our love can restore the strength of another person's innermost character and feelings. When we allow God's love to flow through us, we make a difference. How hard is it to show concern for others? Is there a greater gift we can give to God than to show our love for His children? Make a difference for someone today.

Revelation 18:4

Then I heard another voice from heaven say: "Come out of her, my people, so that you will not share in her sins, so that you will not receive any of her plagues."

People want to fit in. We don't want to be different, yet living like most of the world is more than a mistake: it is a deadly and destructive choice. In this verse, God was speaking of Babylon, which symbolizes the worldly system. He calls His people to come out...to be different. He warns that adopting the ways of the world in opposition to God's directives will bring trouble and grief upon us. Don't accept a system of standards that leads you away from God. Strive to live the way He has told you, and be different. You will also be joyful, secure, confident, hopeful, and at peace.

Mark 6:48b-51

He was about to pass by them, but when they saw Him walking on the lake, they thought He was a ghost. They cried out because they all saw Him and were terrified. Immediately He spoke to them and said, "Take courage! It is I. Don't be afraid." Then He climbed in the boat with them, and the wind died down.

In this account, the disciples had been caught in a storm on the Sea of Galilee. Jesus came toward them walking on the water, but He was in no hurry to go to the struggling disciples. One thing that strikes me here is that He was intending to pass by them. It doesn't seem as if He had planned to stop to help them at all! He didn't see a problem. He knew that the storm, however bad it seemed to them, was going to subside. They would be safe. He was in control. When they cried out to Him, terrified, He immediately spoke to them, climbed in the boat, and calmed the storm. He did this not because they actually needed help, but because they thought they did. Many of the storms of our lives are insignificant in God's eyes except for the fact that we are terrified. When we cry out to Him, He hears our cries...and even though we were already perfectly safe, He climbs in the boat with us anyway.

Matthew 6:34 (The Message)

Give your entire attention to what God is doing right now, and don't get worked up about what may or may not happen tomorrow. God will help you deal with whatever hard things come up when the time comes.

Today is God's gift to us, and it is the only day we are certain we will see upon this earth. Logically, we know that this is true. Still we spend far too much time and energy mentally dealing with problems of tomorrow that more than likely will never occur. Even if they do, worrying about them won't have changed anything. We are in God's hands; our loved ones, our finances, our health, and our dreams are held in the hands of the same God that formed the galaxies and breathed life into every living thing. How can we doubt Him by wasting our time in worry? Trust God. Make this gift—the gift of one more day—count for something.

Psalm 30:5a

For His anger lasts only a moment, but His favor lasts a lifetime.

I have never felt God's anger even though I have deserved to. I know that I have disappointed Him. I believe that His heart has ached because of some of the ridiculous and stupid choices I have made that I will never understand. There were times when He seemed far, far away if I bothered to think of Him at all. However, even when I was wandering around in the wilderness, I knew deep down that He still loved me, and I was welcome to come home. That's one of the many wonderful things about God: He will love us forever. Life outside the boundaries God has set for us is a lonely, miserable, and dangerous place, but we never have to stay there. If you aren't wrapped safely in His arms, hurry home. Your Father is waiting to hold you.

Psalm 30:5b

Weeping may remain for a night, but rejoicing comes in the morning.

I love the morning. I love watching the pink and purple hues grow into an orange glow until the sun shines on everything around me. I love seeing the blankets of fog lift slowly from the hills and valleys. I love hearing the birds welcome the day with their songs. For me, morning signals a new beginning, a fresh start, another chance. Each day that we live brings us healing, comfort, courage, and forgiveness. Sometimes our nights seem to last almost forever, but we are promised that the night will end. Our grief, our remorse, and our fears will pass. God has brought us this far. He won't abandon us ever. There is joy for us in the morning—every morning.

Mark 10:21

Jesus looked at him and loved him. "One thing you lack," He said. "Go, sell everything you have and give to the poor, and you will have treasure in heaven. Then come, follow me."

Jesus' instructions saddened the rich young man. He wanted to inherit the kingdom of God, but he wasn't willing to give up his wealth for it. There was something more important to him than following Jesus. Our Lord won't ask us to give up everything we own to follow Him, but we do have to give up something. We have to give up our self-will. We have to give up our love of the things of this world. We have to give up whatever comes between us and His will for us. In the process, we also can give up our fears, our worries, our heartache, and our guilt. He wants us--broken though we are--and when we follow Him, He takes the broken pieces of our lives and makes us whole.

1 Corinthians 2:9 KJV

But as it is written, Eye hath not seen, nor ear heard, neither have entered into the heart of man, the things which God hath prepared for them that love him.

The place God has prepared is beyond our greatest expectations and our wildest dreams. It is more wonderful than our imaginations can conceive! In all the times I have read this verse or heard it spoken, until recently I had concentrated on the first part. The last part, though--the last part is the most wonderful of all. He didn't prepare this place of splendor for those who gave or did or accomplished the most in this world. He prepared this place for those who love Him, and how could we not? How could we not love the One who created us, redeemed us, watches over us, provides for us, protects us, defends us, rains blessings down upon us, and will love us forever? Loving Him secures eternal life in a place beyond description...and loving Him the easiest thing in the world.

Proverbs 3:5

Trust in the Lord with all your heart and lean not on your own understanding.

We want to understand things. When we are toddlers, our favorite question is, "Why?" As we get older, we want to believe that there is a good reason for everything that happens, and we search for answers. Many times, there aren't any; and we come face to face with the realities of failure, sickness, betrayal, separation, and untimely death. This is when we must realize that we are in a place where we always needed to be—trusting God. Sometimes we just don't understand, and we can make no sense of what is happening in our lives. All any of us can do is remember that God loves us more than we are capable of understanding. As we spend time in His presence, He will give us peace to accept what we cannot understand.

1 Samuel 30:6

David was greatly distressed because the men were talking of stoning him; each one was bitter in spirit because of his sons and daughters. But David found strength in the Lord his God.

David was in the middle of a great calamity. While he and his army had gone to fight enemies, the Amalekites had raided their homes and carried off their wives, sons, and daughters. His men were speaking of stoning him and were bitter in their spirits. There are many ways David could have dealt with these tragic events. He chose to lean on the Lord. He asked God for guidance and trusted Him to lead him on the right path. The results were all he could have hoped for. (Read it for yourself). Whatever calamity--big or small--intrudes upon our lives, we have the power to choose how we respond. We can be like David's men--vengeful and bitter, or we can be like David--leaning on God, His strength, and His guidance. Only when we choose to trust in God can we hope for the restoration of our joy and peace. I hope you have a wonderful day, finding your strength in the Lord your God.

Philippians 3:10,11

I want to know Christ and the power of His resurrection and the fellowship of sharing in His sufferings, becoming like Him in his death, and so, somehow, to attain to the resurrection from the dead.

It's easy to fall into the trap of thinking in the moment. We occupy our minds with the desires of the present and don't leave room to think about things that will matter for all eternity. Paul's goals were lofty. He wanted to know Christ personally and experience His resurrection power. He wanted to be a partner with Christ even if it meant suffering and dying. He wanted and expected to be with Christ for eternity. These goals should be ours…and they should not be for some future time. They are goals for today. Knowing Christ better and better, experiencing His power and even His sufferings--these are the things that matter. These are the things that will give us peace and joy in this life and throughout eternity. Don't waste precious time on worthless things. Spend it striving to be more like Him.

Philippians 4:13

I can do everything through Him who gives me strength.

Do you ever feel too weak to deal with what is happening in your life? If you are like me, there have been times when you thought God was mistaken about what you could bear. There are events in our lives--times of regret, grief, sickness, and disappointment--that would level us if we faced them on our own. The good news is we never have to. We have the power of Almighty God, the creator of all life, working in our behalf. Never doubt that He loves you more than you will ever understand, and He is in control of every part of your life that you have given over to Him. No matter what you face, God will see to it that you come through stronger, more dedicated, and more determined to finish your race...and finish it with flying colors. This is a promise from the One who holds you in His hands and in His heart.

Ephesians 4:29

Do not let any unwholesome talk come out of your mouths, but only what is helpful for building others up according to their needs, that it may benefit those who listen.

Christians know that cursing and vulgarity should have no place in their lives. Many, though, are quick to find fault and criticize others. Actually, few of us could say that we always say things that build others up. There are times when we accidentally (or purposely) make a comment that doesn't help anyone. Paul warns us to be mindful of others' needs and careful what we say. One of our goals as Christians should be to make others feel better and to help them realize how precious they are to God. We can't do that if we are finding fault or criticizing. Make it a point to build up someone today. It will help a brother or sister, make you feel better, and please the King of Kings. Everybody wins when we are careful what we say!

Luke 19:3-5

He (Zacchaeus) wanted to see who Jesus was, but being a short man he could not, because of the crowd. So he ran ahead and climbed a sycamore-fig tree to see Him, since Jesus was coming that way. When Jesus reached the spot, He looked up and said to him, "Zacchaeus, come down immediately. I must stay at your house today."

This would be a heart-breaking account if it were not for Zacchaeus' determination. He was short; the crowd was large. It would have been easy to give up and let Jesus pass him by, but look what he would have missed. Jesus went home with him! Even today people can miss out on a close relationship with Jesus for similar reasons. They look to their natural abilities instead of God's supernatural power to work in their lives. When things look impossible, they give up. In addition, they let the multitudes and the cares of this world crowd in, keeping them from drawing close to Jesus Christ. What is the price they pay? They miss having the Lord of all coming to stay with them, bringing with Him joy and peace. I hope you are determined today to let nothing come between you and a closer walk with Jesus.

Psalm 39:2

But when I was silent and still, not even saying anything good, my anguish increased.

When David wrote this Psalm, he was ill, overcome with the scourge on his life. He had determined that he wouldn't say anything, but he found that being silent made things worse. Then he poured out his heart to God. Calling out to God is what we should do, too. He doesn't expect or want us to keep our feelings pent up inside, and He won't be offended if we tell Him what's in our minds and hearts (He knows anyway). Remember Jesus said, "Come unto me all ye that labor and are heavy laden"? He wasn't talking about carrying too many pounds of stuff around. He wants you to bring your problems to Him. An honest conversation with your Lord and King will make anything look better. Spend some time with Him today and tell Him what's causing you pain. Just remember that when you tell Him what's wrong in your life, you should also thank Him for all the things that are right.

Revelation 3:8

I know your deeds. See, I have placed before you an open door that no one can shut. I know that you have little strength, yet you have kept my word and have not denied my name.

We feel guilty when we fail to measure up to what we expect of ourselves. We should have been stronger, should have tried harder, should have… should have. We sometimes even feel responsible for others' mistakes or pain because in our minds, there was surely something we could have done differently that would have helped. Jesus knows our deeds, and He knows our hearts. He knows we are weak and loves us anyway. He doesn't ask us to move mountains on our own. All He really asks is that we keep His Word, repent when we fail, and acknowledge Him as Lord of our lives and Savior of our souls. The open door to Him is a permanent thing. No one can shut it. We can go to Him anytime for anything and know that He hears and answers our prayers. He is always there lifting us up, cheering us on, applauding our successes, and forgiving our sins. What a wonderful Lord and Master He is!

1 Samuel 2:9 KJV

He will keep the feet of his saints, and the wicked shall be silent in darkness; for by strength shall no man prevail.

What have you accomplished on your own? What problems have you solved or what enemies have you defeated? I hope you answered, "None," for that would be the truth. We haven't conquered anything through our own power…and we don't have to. It is by God's strength that we are able to be victorious through problems that seem insurmountable. It is through His power that we can stand when it seems impossible. God has given us many victories in areas we have not submitted to Him, and He has rescued us when we did not ask Him to. However, it is only when admit our total weakness and trust Him with everything that we can truly prevail. I pray that you recognize Him today not only as your Creator, Redeemer, Savior, Provider, King, and Friend, but also as your only Source of Strength.

Deuteronomy 1:6

The Lord our God said to us at Horeb, "You have stayed long enough at this mountain."

The road to the Promised Land wasn't a direct route for the Israelites. They lacked faith in God and disobeyed Him, and they suffered because of it. However, there came a time for them to move on and claim their promises. All of us have wandered in a desert of disobedience, too; but if we repent, God forgives us. We do not have to stay at the mountain, beating ourselves up and listening to the devil remind us how badly we have failed. That's not what God wants. That's not why Jesus died. If you are still dwelling in the past, circling your mountain of your regret, stop it. You have stayed long enough. God forgives you and loves you. Move on.

John 11:40

Then Jesus said, "Did I not tell you that if you believed, you would see the glory of God?"

When Lazarus became very sick, Mary and Martha sent for Jesus, hoping He would heal their brother. He did not come immediately, and Lazarus died. Jesus did not grant the miracle Mary and Martha had asked for...but when He raised Lazarus from the dead, they received a far greater miracle than they had dreamed. If we believe God is omnipotent and can perform miracles in our lives, then we must also believe that He is omniscient and knows what is best. Could it be that if He answers our prayers in the way we ask, we would miss a greater blessing God has planned for us? He is in control, and we are in His hands. Trust Him. Believe Him. Sometimes trusting and believing also involves waiting--waiting to see His glory.

1 Corinthians 3:6,7

I planted the seed, Apollos watered it, but God made it grow. So neither he who plants nor he who waters is anything, but only God, who makes things grow.

I live in a rural area where many people grow at least a portion of their food. Each year they break ground, plant seeds, and take care of the plants as they grow. They do this believing that the crops will thrive and produce, but the final outcome is really out of their control. When we try to reach others for Christ, we can tell others about Him and try to help them learn and become stronger. We can't, however, make them listen to God as He speaks to their hearts. The depth of the relationship they develop is between them and their God, just as it is for us. Tell others about Christ, help them in whatever way you can, and leave the harvest to God.

Mark 3:20,21

Then Jesus entered a house, and again a crowd gathered, so that He and His disciples were not even able to eat. When His family heard about this, they went to take charge of Him, for they said, "He is out of His mind."

At this point in Jesus' ministry, He had already amazed the crowds with His teaching, cast out demons of all kinds, and healed throngs of people. Crowds followed Him everywhere and gathered in on Him, but His family went to take charge of Him because--get this--they thought He was crazy! This struck me as sad and amusing at the same time, and I wondered how Jesus felt about the whole thing. I think He may have been amused, too. In fact, I can imagine that He even smiled. What they thought didn't change the truth...Jesus knew who He was. He was, and is, the Redeemer of the world, the King of Kings, and God's son. How people perceive us shouldn't change what we think of ourselves, either. We know who we are--we are God's children, joint heirs with Jesus. God loves us dearly. As you go about your day working, shopping, dealing with the cares of the day, don't forget who you are. You are a redeemed, precious, much-loved Child of God.

Psalm 40:2,3a

He lifted me out of the slimy pit, out of the mud and mire; He set my feet on a rock and gave me a firm place to stand. He put a new song in my mouth, a hymn of praise to our God.

God is always willing to rescue us from the slimy pit. Our rescue is not complete, though, until we accept it. If we continue to dwell on the past, we are rejecting the joy that comes through His forgiveness. Satan would like to convince us that we don't deserve to be forgiven, that we are second-class citizens, and that we should go around in sackcloth and ashes for the rest of our lives. What a lie! God wants us to be filled with joy. He has put a new song in our mouths, for Heaven's sake! We are all rescued, forgiven, much-loved children of the Almighty Creator of the Universe. Open your mouth and sing your songs of joy.

Isaiah 46:4

Even to your old age and gray hairs I am He, I am He who will sustain you. I have made you and I will carry you: I will sustain you and will rescue you.

I am not an expert on old age although I am becoming one too quickly. I do know that we live in a throwaway society where people in their "golden years" (strange expression) are not revered and respected as they deserve. Unfortunately, many older people are made to feel worthless, and they spend their final years miserably. And then--and then--there are the older Christians who maintain their joy through trials because they love the Lord. They know that the Creator of the Universe values them dearly. They are assured that God has a plan and purpose for their lives down to the very last day. Those of us who have been blessed to watch one of God's older servants have seen His promises in action. We have seen that He really does sustain, carry, and rescue those who put their trust in Him throughout their days. Their lives of peace and joy testify to God's faithfulness. I don't like some of the changes that are taking place in me as I grow older, but I am confident that He who sees a sparrow fall will care for me all of my days.

Lamentations 3:57,58

You came near when I called you, and you said, "Do not fear." O, Lord, you took up my case; you redeemed my life.

I marvel when I consider the number of times God has come to my aid. He has rescued me from more problems and perils than I can count. He has willingly taken burdens from me over and over--often the same one that I had snatched back for another attempt to do it my way. I can't explain it, and I don't deserve it...but God simply does not give up on me. He doesn't give up on you, either. We are His beloved children. He is always there, ready to draw near when we call, calm our fears, and fight our battles. He even sent Jesus to pay the price for our sins and redeem us from eternal punishment. What more could He do to convince us that He will love us forever?

Acts 7:55,59,60

But Stephen, full of the Holy Spirit, looked up to heaven and saw the glory of God, and Jesus standing at the right hand of God... While they were stoning him, Stephen prayed, "Lord Jesus, receive my spirit." Then he fell on his knees and cried out, "Lord, do not hold this sin against them." When he had said this, he fell asleep.

Stephen, filled with the Holy Spirit, did great wonders and performed miraculous signs among the people. The Jewish leaders wanted to silence Him, and so they brought false witnesses against him and stoned him to death. As a child, I thought this account had a bad ending. I wanted Jesus to zap the bad guys and save Stephen from the mob. But I see now that Stephen had a mighty role to play in the spread of the Gospel, and his death at the hands of the Jews was a key part. Stephen was willing. He was willing to be used however God wanted, willing to die rather than deny Jesus, and willing to forgive those who killed him. As Stephen fulfilled the role planned for Him from the beginning of time, Heaven opened and he saw the glory of God. Whatever God asks us to do, however hard it may seem, God will give us the strength. If we are faithful, we can end our days here like Stephen. We can see God's glory as Heaven opens for us.

Isaiah 50:4

The Sovereign Lord has given me an instructed tongue, to know the word that sustains the weary. He wakens me morning by morning, wakens my ear to listen like one being taught.

What's the first thing you do when you wake up in the morning? Do you grumble at the alarm clock as your mind floods with thoughts of the tasks facing you? Isaiah awoke to listen to the Lord. He spent time with His creator expecting that God would speak to his heart. Because Isaiah was open to the Lord's teaching, he was able to help those around him. He had the words to lift up the weary, sad, and downtrodden because God had given him those words. God will give us an instructed tongue, too, and the words to lift up someone who needs comfort or encouragement. Even though we aren't aware of it at the time, He places within us the ability to help others when we spend time with Him. When you wake up in the morning, try to push aside the cares of this temporary earthly life. Listen instead for God's voice, instructing you and reminding you how much He loves you.

1 Samuel 7:12

Then Samuel took a stone and set it up between Mizpa and Shen. He named it Ebenezer (stone of help) saying, "Thus far has the Lord helped us."

The Philistines were advancing toward the Israelites. However, the Lord thundered with a loud thunder against the Philistines and threw them into panic. Then the Israelites were able to rush out and destroy them. There would be other battles for God's people, but Samuel wanted to honor God for bringing them "thus far." He set aside some time to mark their victory and honor God. What about us? God has also brought us safely through many battles, hasn't He? There will be other trials and troubles for us to face and conquer. Maybe God will give us instant victory, or maybe our victory will come through battle. He, however, will see us through. Spend some time remembering your victories, and honor God for His faithfulness. Thus far has the Lord helped us; He will see us the rest of the way. Rejoice, child of God. It's true!

Isaiah 62:6b,7

You who call on the Lord, give yourselves no rest, and give Him no rest till He establishes Jerusalem and makes her the praise of the earth.

How diligent are we in our attempts to move the hands of God? Do we come before His throne regularly? And when we don't see His answers, do we give up? Isaiah gives us some crucial advice here: don't do a halfway job when you petition God, and don't give up until you have His answer. We should be totally dedicated. Praying is a serious matter. Only when we get to Heaven will we know the lives that were changed, the people that were healed, the tragedies that were averted, and the souls that were saved because of our prayers. Spend some real time before His throne today whatever you have to give up to do it.

2 Corinthians 10:12

We do not dare to classify or compare ourselves with some who commend themselves. When they measure themselves by themselves and compare themselves with themselves, they are not wise.

It is easy to fall into the trap of comparing ourselves with others. We are bombarded on every side with the idea that we should want hair, skin, body, or possessions like someone else. This thinking is a waste of precious time, to say the least; however, comparing ourselves to others spiritually is much worse. Each person has his or her own talents, strengths, and gifts from God. We cannot be and should not want to be like any other person. We may learn from others, and we may respect the way they live their lives. No person, though, is our example. Jesus Himself is. God made only one you. Celebrate your uniqueness as you strive to be all He made you to be.

John 5:6 KJV

When Jesus saw him lie, and knew that he had been now a long time in that case, He saith unto him, "Wilt thou be made whole?"

In this passage, Jesus was speaking to a lame man at the pool at Bethesda. It is interesting that Jesus asked him if he wanted to be made whole as if it were a choice he could make. I don't understand how or why God grants healing to some although I know from personal experience that He does. Physical wholeness is a wonderful gift from God, yet there is something greater: wholeness of mind, emotions, and spirit. When Jesus died to ransom us, He made us whole. He paid the price for our sins and daily holds out His arms to us to comfort, console, and carry us through. Whether we accept or not is a choice we do make. And so the question is for us, too: "Wilt thou be made whole?" I pray that your answer is 'yes,' and that you spend time in His Presence today, allowing His healing power to work within you.

Luke 22:46

"Why are you sleeping?" He asked them. "Get up and pray so that you will not fall into temptation."

Few people make a conscious decision to get tangled up in a web of sin and destruction. Their entrapment is often a gradual process. It may begin with seemingly harmless actions and progress as they sleep through warning signs that could rescue them. We can't afford to be so caught up in the comings and goings of everyday life that we wander off on the wrong path, oblivious to the consequences. Jesus admonished His disciples to get up and pray, to be alert, and to ask God for strength and guidance. There are millions of pitfalls waiting for someone who is unaware. Stay awake; stay alert; stay close to your Creator and King through your prayers.

James 4:2b

You do not have because you do not ask God.

Could we count the many times have we struggled through a problem or a task on our own because we weren't willing to ask for help? Too often we get in our "I-can-do-it-myself" mode, and we make our lives much harder because of it. The same thing is true in our spiritual lives. A lie from Satan causes us to think we should be strong enough to handle our problems and deal with our troubles. We aren't. We need God. He is willing to help us with anything at any time, but He stands back if we insist on doing it ourselves. God is not just our creator and master; He is our father. He loves us. He dotes on us. He would do anything for us. He gave His only Son to save us, didn't He? Though there are millions of His children on this earth, He watches over each of us and longs to be involved in each individual life. When you are tired, hurt, worried, weary, tempted, grieving, angry--when you just can't do it by yourself--ask Him. Keep on asking. Give yourselves no rest until you see His mighty power at work in your situation and feel His mighty presence in your life.

Psalm 62:8

Trust in Him at all times, O people; pour out your hearts to him, for God is our refuge.

Think of your heart as a vessel. It can only contain so much. If we hold on to our past--the mistakes, betrayal, injustice, disappointment, grief, and all the other things that cause us pain--we will eventually choke out the good things in our lives. If we are willing to empty our hearts before God, He will fill us with His joy and peace. He wants to carry our burdens; He wants to give us hope in this life and for the life to come. He won't, however, snatch our troubles from our white-knuckled clutches and cram hope down our throats. We have to accept His gift. Do your heart a favor. Make time for God today. Pour out your heart to Him and make room for the comfort, joy, peace, and love Christ died to give you.

Isaiah 58:9

Then you will call, and the Lord will answer; you will cry for help and He will say: Here am I.

We humans learn at an early age that we usually have to wait our turn whether we like it or not. Neither our families, our friends, nor our coworkers can respond the instant we ask them to. Even when we need a dentist or doctor and are willing to pay, we have to make an appointment and wait. Not so with God. He isn't too busy running the Universe or keeping the sun in place and the planets in orbit. We don't have to wait in line while He listens to millions of others. He hears us... and answers us as soon as we call. He is always there, ready to listen and ready to act on our behalf. Don't struggle with troubles and trials on your own. Don't delay in seeking Him. Call on Him and expect to hear Him speak to your heart, "Here am I."

Genesis 18:13,14

Then the Lord said to Abraham, "Why did Sarah laugh and say, 'Will I really have a child, now that I am old?' Is anything too hard for the Lord? I will return to you at the appointed time next year, and Sarah will have a son."

Sarah didn't believe God. She had put limits on His power and laughed at the idea that she could still have a child at ninety years of age. We can understand her; after all, in our natural world it was impossible. But--here's the good part--our God is not of this world. He is above all kingdoms and all powers. He is not bound by any rules of nature or by what man says is possible. Some of you are facing hard things--problems with health, relationships, or finances--and you are unsure about the future. Never limit God's ability to grant your total healing. He created a miracle of life in Sarah; He can fix your brokenness, too. Trust, wait, and be joyful, for you are a Child of the Omnipotent God.

Hebrews 10:35

So do not throw away your confidence; it will be richly rewarded.

Our confidence in God--our faith that He has done, can do, and will do all He has promised--is the foundation of our lives as Christians. We are warned here to guard our confidence, to let nothing or nobody cause us to waver in our faith. Satan would love more than anything to fill us with doubt that God loves us and will take care of us through whatever rough paths and stormy seas we are bound to encounter. Our enemy wants to fill us with fear and dread. He wants us to miss the joy and blessings God has for His children. Our minds cannot even imagine the reward He has waiting for us when we leave this world; however, here on earth we can have overwhelming peace and joy that comes by knowing that Almighty God, Creator of the Universe, will never, never fail us. We are His sons and daughters, and He adores us. Never doubt it--not for an instant.

Psalm 37:23,24

If the Lord delights in a man's way, He makes his steps firm; though he stumble, he will not fall, for the Lord upholds him with His hand.

Some people expect Christians to be perfect. In fact, Christians often expect that of themselves. Perhaps it is because Christ led a perfect, sinless life, and some part of us thinks we should be able to do the same. This verse reassures us because it shows that God can delight in our way even though we stumble. That's what it says! We bring Him joy by being dedicated and diligent, committed to following the path He has set before us. He doesn't ask for perfection. When we stumble, God Himself holds us up to keep us from falling. How great is that! He doesn't sit in Heaven and shake His head in disgust when we fail. He doesn't say, "They've had all the chances I intend to give them." No, He gently reaches down, puts us back on the right path, and says, "Try again, My Child. You can be all I called you to be." And you know what? With God's help, we can.

Philippians 1:6 (The Message)

There has never been the slightest doubt in my mind that the God who started this great work in you would keep at it and bring it to a flourishing finish on the very day Christ Jesus appears.

We can be assured of two wonderful truths from this verse. First, God is not going to give up on us. He didn't reach out to us, calling to our hearts, only to abandon us down the road. Even if we wander away down a path of destruction, God will continue to work in our lives to bring us back. Second, He won't be finished with this work until Jesus comes to take us home. This means that we will never be perfect or self-sufficient. We will always need God's help in staying on the course. He has given us free will, though, and He requires our cooperation. My prayer for you is that you are cooperating with God. Listen to His warnings and His instructions. Let Him keep you on the smooth, straight road that leads directly to His throne...and enjoy all the blessings obedience brings.

Isaiah 64:4,5a

Since ancient times no one has heard, no ear has perceived, no eye has seen any God besides you, who acts on behalf of those who wait for Him. You come to the help of those who gladly do right, who remember your ways.

God is amazing. Even though He has the power to create or destroy a universe with a word, He is still concerned and involved with each of us. Think about that for a minute. God actually singles out each of us and acts in our behalf! He knows every trial, every betrayal, every heartache, and every failure we have ever experienced...and He is willing to reach down, rescue us, and heal our brokenness. He does this because He loves us immeasurably. How can we ever return His love? We return His love by obeying Him and remembering the way He has set before us. As you go about your day today, be aware that whatever you are facing, God is busy working the situation for your good. His hands are moving...and they are moving just for you.

Job 33:14

For God does speak—now one way, now another—though man may not perceive it.

Do we really listen for God to speak to us? Sometimes, we ignore Him because He isn't saying what we expect or want. We pray to Him, asking Him to give us guidance or to act in our behalf. Then we wait and watch for Him to answer us in a way we have decided that He should. It is even possible that we may wait months and years for an answer He gave us in the beginning. God hears every thought, every prayer, and every plea. He answers us each time. He speaks to us through His written Word, through songs, and through others. Sometimes, He speaks directly to our hearts. Don't miss out on what your Heavenly Father wants to tell you. Be open and listen for His voice.

Luke 13:10-13

On a Sabbath Jesus was teaching in one of the synagogues, and a woman was there who had been crippled by a spirit for eighteen years. She was bent over and could not straighten up at all. When Jesus saw her, He called her forward and said to her, "Woman, you are set free from your infirmity." Then He put His hands on her, and immediately she straightened up and praised God.

The woman in this account was under attack by a spirit. She was crippled and helpless, but Jesus saw her, called her forward, and set her free. Because He touched her, she no longer was bent under her burden. We assume that this was physical, but I can tell you without any doubt that Satan also attacks to cripple our hopes, our dreams, our determination, and our wills. The Bible teaches us that we are in a spiritual warfare, and at times we all have been bent over from those attacks. Praise God, we have the same privilege and the same hope as the woman in this account. We can come into His presence, bowed low with disappointment, sorrow, pain, and discouragement...and have every confidence that He will touch us and set us free. I hope that you are standing straight and tall today, walking by your Savior's side.

Acts 9:21a,22

All those who heard him (Saul) were astonished and asked, "Isn't he the man who raised havoc in Jerusalem among those who call on this (Jesus') name?"...Yet Saul grew more and more powerful and baffled the Jews living in Damascus by proving that Jesus is the Christ.

The change in Saul/Paul astonished those who knew him. He had met the Master, and his life was turned upside down, inside out. God changed him completely. This was obvious to everyone. We have not persecuted Christians in our past as Saul did, and we may not be called to travel throughout the world spreading the Gospel as he was. Still, when God saved us, He changed us, too. Our faith in Jesus Christ should be obvious by the way we talk and act. It should be obvious by the way we treat others and the way we live our lives. It should be obvious by our strength and our joy. If anyone is ever astonished because of us, let it be because of the mighty difference Christ has made within us.

1 Samuel 17:37a

The Lord who delivered me from the paw of the lion and the paw of the bear will deliver me from the hand of this Philistine.

David was confident that the Lord would deliver him from the hand of Goliath. Why? It was because he had a history with God. He had faced other challenges, and the Lord had brought him through with victory. While others looked at the size of the giant, David looked at the size of his God. We need David's spirit of faith and trust in our lives today. We need to face every trial remembering the times God has delivered us in the past. How many times have we been where there seemed to be no escape...yet God has made a way? Nothing is impossible with God. There is no problem, no circumstance, no trial in our lives that is bigger than He is. Whatever may be wrong in your life today, look to your God. You have a history with Him. He won't fail you this time, either.

1 Corinthians 6:19,20

Do you not know that your body is a temple of the Holy Spirit, who is in you, whom you have received from God? You are not your own; you were bought at a price. Therefore honor God with your body.

In this section of Scripture, Paul was talking about sexual immorality, but there are other ways we can dishonor God with our bodies. To honor Him, we must do what we should to maintain the health that we have. We should develop our skills. We should try to make our hearts a place of love and peace. We should clean up our lives by getting rid of the junk--the strife, jealousy, worry, selfishness, or anything else that dishonors Him and weakens our witness. The its-my-life mentality is deception from the devil. We were bought with a price, and the Lord God Almighty is our Master. Do an inventory of your life. Ask Him to show you what needs to be cast out as junk and to give you the strength to do it. Give the Holy Spirit a peaceful, loving place in which to live.

Exodus 14:21,22

Then Moses stretched out his hand over the sea, and all that night the Lord drove the sea back with a strong east wind and turned it into dry land. The waters were divided, and the Israelites went through the sea on dry ground, with a wall of water on their right and on their left.

With this miracle, God rescued the Israelites from certain destruction. Their enemy, Pharoh's army, was in fast pursuit; the sea blocked their way forward. God could have transported them instantly across the sea, but they had to walk through. They had to face their fears and trust God to see them safely to the other side. In the same way, there are times in our lives when we have to walk through...and when it looks as though the waters could engulf us at any moment. We must have faith and believe that our God can and will protect us and rescue from any enemy we face. It's significant that the Israelites walked through on dry ground. They didn't have to slop around in the mud and muck and take parts of the seabed with them. God made a path, and He made it easy. My prayer for you is that you will trust God to part the waters for you whenever they are too deep...and that you will arrive safely on the other side with clean sandals.

Proverbs 21:30

There is no wisdom, no insight, no plan that can succeed against the Lord.

Have you ever been determined to make a plan work when nothing seemed to fall into place? I have...and I can tell you that no matter how much I may have plotted or schemed, my plan was not successful if God was against it. I am grateful for those failures, for I realize it was God's hand rescuing me. He loves me so much that He would move mountains to keep me from destroying myself. He loves you that much, too. Whenever things don't happen as you planned, believe that God is at work…and His plan for you is better than anything you could have ever dreamed.

Revelation 3:9

I will make those who are of the synagogue of Satan, who claim to be Jews though they are not, but are liars—I will make them come and fall down at your feet and acknowledge that I have loved you.

I want those who know me to know that I am a Christian. I want to live my life in such a way that my love for Jesus shows. Satan and those who are trapped in his snare want to bring Christians down. They point out every fault and chink in our armor (real or imagined), thinking that in this way they can diminish Jesus. This verse contains a powerful truth: Satan's followers, who have worked so hard to damage and destroy our Christian witness, will one day have to fall at our feet and acknowledge that Jesus loves us. The best part of all, though, is that even if they didn't acknowledge it, it would still be true. Jesus loves us!

Matthew 8:14

When Jesus came into Peter's house, He saw Peter's mother-in-law lying in bed with a fever. He touched her hand and the fever left her, and she got up and began to wait on Him.

Peter's mother-in-law was sick in bed, unable to function. When Jesus touched her and made her well, what did she do? She got up and began to serve Him. There have been and will be seasons in our lives when it is hard for us to function, too. It might be because of illness as in her case.

It might also be because of discouragement, sorrow, guilt, confusion, or just plain weariness. Jesus has been faithful to touch our lives as He did hers, and we have been able to continue when we thought we couldn't. What should our response be? We shouldn't just plop down and breathe a sigh of relief. We have been rescued, healed, and delivered for a reason--because He has a purpose for us here. We should get up and serve Him.

Proverbs 10:25 NKJV

When the whirlwind passes by, the wicked is no more, but the righteous has an everlasting foundation.

All of us face whirlwinds in our lives at times. We have all gone through periods when our faith was tested, and we may have even doubted our ability to survive. One of the differences between Christians and those who don't claim Christ is this: we will overcome. We may stand in the middle of a storm, but we will stand. When the storm has passed, we will still be standing. Because we have been washed in the blood of Christ and have put on His righteousness, our foundation is firm, secure, and everlasting. No matter what whirlwinds may come against you today, rest assured that God will keep you standing through them all.

1 Samuel 18:14

In everything he (David) did, he had great success because the Lord was with him.

The list of successes in David's life is impressive. He was the youngest born to a family of shepherds, yet he rose to be the greatest king in Israel's history. He commanded a great army and won so many battles that the people sang songs about his victories. David performed mighty feats and defeated foes with little effort whenever he consulted God first and followed His instructions. Too often, we exercise our right to fail by not consulting God. He is willing to help us with every problem, no matter how big or how small. We can be victorious over every foe if we just do as He says. Ask Him to help you with all your decisions and listen when He speaks to your heart. You, too, will have great success because the Lord will be with you.

Zephaniah 3:17

The Lord your God is with you, He is mighty to save. He will take great delight in you, He will quiet you with his love, He will rejoice over you with singing.

What comfort this verse contains! The beginning is no surprise to Christians. We all believe He is with us and that He is able to save us by His mighty power. That's what Christians believe. But the idea that He delights in me is almost more than I can take in! He quiets me with His love, giving me peace in all situations. He even rejoices over me with singing! How can this be so? He is the King of the Universe! He made everything and everyone who has ever existed or ever will exist. How can He delight in and rejoice over one insignificant person? The wonderful truth is, Brothers and Sisters, that there is no such thing as an insignificant person in God's eyes. He adores us--each and every one of us. Spend some time with Him today. Let Him sing your heart a song of joy.

John 14:4-6

(Jesus speaking) "You know the way to the place where I am going." Thomas said to Him, "Lord, we don't know where you are going,

so how can we know the way?" Jesus answered, "I am the way and the truth and the life. No one comes to the Father except through me."

When I was a child, and someone told me that we were going somewhere, I was confident that we were. I didn't worry about the details. I trusted that my dad, mom, or whoever was taking me could get me there. About all I had to do was get in the car and stay there. In the first few verses of John 14, Jesus explained that He has prepared a beautiful place for us and that He will take us there. We don't have to worry about where this home is. We don't need to have a map. Jesus Himself is the Way. Our only responsibility is to trust Him with a child-like faith and stay where we are supposed to be—by His side.

Job 42:8,10

"So now take seven bulls and seven rams and go to my servant Job and sacrifice a burnt offering for yourselves. My servant Job will pray for you, and I will accept his prayer and not deal with you according to your folly. You have not spoken of me what is right, as my servant Job has."...After Job had prayed for his friends, the Lord made him prosperous and gave him twice as much as he had before.

The Lord was angry with three of Job's friends. They had not spoken what was true about God and had tried to convince Job that God had turned against him because of his sin. Isn't it interesting that God told them to go to Job and that <u>Job</u> would pray for them? The burnt offerings showed their repentance, but it was Job's prayer for them that God accepted. We need to seek others' forgiveness when we wrong them; we also need to forgive and pray for others who have wronged us. Do you think God would have restored all the things Job had lost if he had refused to pray for his friends? AFTER he had prayed, the Lord made him prosperous again. We need to seek forgiveness from others and ask for their prayers…and we need to forgive and pray for those who have hurt us.

Psalm 59:11

But do not kill them, O Lord our shield, or my people will forget.

The word "them" in this verse refers to the enemies of David, the evildoers, the bloodthirsty men who lay in wait and conspired against him. How easy it would have been for David to ask God to annihilate them, to wipe them from the face of the earth! This might be what we would ask for. We would like for all our problems to simply disappear, zapped into nothingness. David wisely realized that hardships serve to remind us how much we need God, who is and always will be our only source, our only refuge. No matter how difficult our lives may seem at times at times, nothing is as tragic as our lives would be if we forgot God.

Joshua 3:2-4a

After three days the officers went throughout the camp, giving orders to the people. "When you see the ark of the covenant of the Lord your God, and the priests, who are Levites, carrying it, you are to move out from your positions and follow it. Then you will know which way to go since you have never been this way before."

Imagine yourself in an unfamiliar, hostile, dangerous land. You have no idea where you are or which way to go. This was the case of the Israelites, but the Creator of the Universe, the Lord of everything, had promised to show them the way. They were told to follow the Ark of the Covenant, which contained the stone tablets (God's covenant). God's Presence was there as He met with Moses at the Mercy Seat. When the Israelites followed the Ark, they were symbolically remaining in His Presence and following His Word. Every day that we live, we are traveling on a path we haven't traveled before, and many times it is treacherous and painful. God has given us everything we need to make it through, but if we are to travel safely and fearlessly, we must remain in His Presence and follow His Word. I pray that God gives you strength and courage as you keep your eyes on Him

Psalm 149:4a

For the Lord takes delight in His people.

To me, there's nothing like a little child to fill the heart with delight. Every move, every word can be a source of pleasure and joy. That's how God looks at His children. We don't have to achieve great things to please Him. He takes delight in us when we are kind to others and willing to help them. He takes delight in us when we refuse to compromise to fit in with the world. He takes delight in us when we are willing to testify about His Kingship in our lives…not with words only but with everything we do and say. I pray that God can smile as He looks down on each of us and say, "That's my child." Determine today to make your choices so that God can take delight in you.

Malachi 4:2

But for you that revere my name, the Sun of righteousness will rise with healing in his wings; and you will go out and leap like calves released from the stall.

Jesus is my hero. He took the punishment for my sins and saved me from eternal separation. That fact alone is greater than words can describe, but He wasn't finished saving me. No matter what happens in my life that threatens me, weakens me, wounds me, or attempts to destroy me, Jesus is there. In my mind, I can see Him rising like the sun with His radiant goodness overcoming every evil force. He spreads His protective wings over me, concealing me and healing me. I am free from guilt, despair, and the sentence I deserve. How could I not leap for joy? He does the same for all who believe in Him...and aren't you thankful? He's your hero, too!

Philippians 1:18b,19

Yes, and I will continue to rejoice, for I know that through your prayers and the help given by the Spirit of Jesus Christ, what has happened to me will turn out for my deliverance.

Paul was in prison when he wrote this, in chains because he was a follower of Christ. His hardships, as difficult as they were, were not enough to keep him from rejoicing. He had every confidence that he would be delivered from his captivity through the prayers of fellow Christians and the help of the Holy Spirit. Bad things happen to us, too, and we can find ourselves in chains. These chains might have been caused by our own mistakes, or others might have caused them. All have the power to destroy our joy if we let them, for their power is greater than any made of metal. They are not greater than our Lord. We need to ask for the prayers of others, look to the help of the Holy Spirit, and continue to rejoice, knowing beyond any doubt that we will be delivered and set free. That's why Jesus came to earth and gave His life. Remember? He came to set us free...and he whom the Son sets free is free indeed.

Psalm 51:1

Have mercy on me, O God, according to your unfailing love; according to your great compassion blot out my transgressions.

If you haven't read Psalm 51 lately, I encourage you to do so. This was written at the lowest point in David's life. He had committed adultery with Bathsheba and, in effect, had murdered her husband. Yet he knew that there was hope for him--hope for forgiveness and restoration. There was hope because of God's mercy, His unfailing love, and His great compassion. God hasn't changed. There is always hope for us, too. Don't allow yourself to be burdened with the guilt of your sin. Give it to God...your merciful, loving, and compassionate Father...and feel the indescribable joy of knowing that your sins are gone.

Psalm 51:13

Then I will teach transgressors your ways, and sinners will turn back to you.

David expected a cleansing and renewal from God's hands. His forgiveness and restoration were gifts given freely by God the Father. There was, however, something David wanted to do in return. He wanted to help others caught in Satan's web of sin and misery. We should always have a heart to help others--help them by testifying to God's great compassion, His love, and His forgiveness. We must help others see that God is merciful and that He wants nothing more than to make them whole again. Don't be satisfied as long as someone you know is burdened with guilt. Help him or her understand that God's love is great, and He is willing to cleanse and renew each heart.

Isaiah 51:11

The ransomed of the Lord will return. They will enter Zion with singing; everlasting joy will crown their heads. Gladness and joy will overtake them, and sorrow and sighing will flee away.

Probably none of us has ever been captured and taken away to a foreign country as the Israelites were, but there are many things that hold people captive--even Christians. God's promise to us is that we will be ransomed and returned, freed from things that cause us grief, sadness, pain, and sufferings of all kinds. He will keep us from drowning in any of the mucky pits Satan has dug for us. And look at how we survive! We won't be whimpering, all scratched up and bruised in a muddy mess. We will be singing, crowned with everlasting joy! We won't have to search for gladness and joy. In fact, we couldn't avoid them if we tried, for they will overtake us. This Scripture is not just for the Israelites of old or for us some time in the future. Even now, God wants to rescue us and fill us with gladness and joy any time we draw near to Him.

Romans 8:28

And we know that in all things God works for the good of those who love him, who have been called according to His purpose.

Some people read this to mean that all bad things happen for a reason as part of God's master plan. That would have to mean that God caused our trouble and grief, and I don't believe that for a moment. Satan is a powerful force on this earth; men by the millions listen to him and cause others untold turmoil and pain. However, God is at work in the lives of those who love Him to bring something good from even the worst of circumstances and to equip us to fulfill His purpose for our lives. Our hope is not that we will escape every bad thing in life, but that our God is able to bring us through them all. I pray that every trial in your life will become a decisive victory.

John 6:3

Then Jesus went up on a mountainside and sat down with his disciples.

When I think about this verse, I feel something close to envy. I so wish I could climb the hill behind my house and sit down with Jesus! Then a still, small voice reminds me that I can...anytime I choose. Jesus is always beside us, always willing to spend time with us. He doesn't intrude or force Himself upon us; He knocks on the door of our hearts and waits for an invitation. When we open that door wide and truly seek His company, His Spirit within us fills us with indescribable peace and joy. Jesus told His disciples later that He was going away but would send the Comforter who would be with us forever. He physically left the earth, but His Spirit remains to teach us the truth and give us an abundant life...remember? That's why He came. Make sure the door to your heart is open wide, and spend some special time with Him today.

Deuteronomy 30:19,20a

This day I call heaven and earth as witnesses against you that I have set before you life and death, blessings, and curses. Now choose life, so that you and your children may live and that you may love the Lord your God, listen to His voice, and hold fast to Him. For the Lord is your life.

It's hard to understand why anyone would choose to live his or her life apart from God. The sad fact is that millions and millions do choose death and curses, not only for themselves but also for their children. God doesn't force Himself upon anyone. He may reach out, touch, prod, and send others to help turn the hearts of men to Him; but in the end, we choose. As Christians, we have made our decision. We chose Him--we chose life--a glorious life filled with love, joy, and peace. It's a done deal, and aren't you glad!

Acts 27:23-25

Last night an angel of the God whose I am and whom I serve stood beside me and said, "Do not be afraid, Paul. You must stand trial before Caesar; and God has graciously given you the lives of all who sail with you." So keep up your courage, men, for I have faith in God that it will happen just as He told me.

If you read the rest of this account, you find that it was not smooth sailing for Paul and the others. Their ship was driven by winds for fourteen nights. It eventually broke apart, and the sailors wanted to kill Paul and the other prisoners. Paul was able to keep his courage throughout because he knew he could trust God's Word. God spoke to Paul through an angel. He speaks to us through the Scriptures, He speaks to us through others, and sometimes He speaks directly to our hearts. Our strength, our hope, and our joy lie in believing what God says. He will never fail us, never leave us, and never stop loving us. Even if it seems our ship is breaking apart, God will carry us safely through our storm. We can ride it out in unbelieving terror, or we can sail calmly on with faith and inner peace, knowing that the seas of life are subject to His commands.

Luke 1:37 KJV

For with God nothing shall be impossible.

The angel had just told Mary two seemingly impossible things: Mary's cousin Elizabeth would have a child in her old age, and Mary herself, though a virgin, would bear the Son of God. Their situations were very different. Elizabeth had prayed for a child; for Mary, it was the farthest thing from her mind. But they were both devout and upright in the sight of God, and God's favor was upon them. Many of us read this verse in passing, accepting its truth for Mary and Elizabeth but not applying it to ourselves. The Bible teaches that God is the same yesterday, today, and forever...and that He is no respecter of persons. Applying it to our lives, it means that God can fix anything. He can mend our brokenness and bring life where there was none. He can heal bodies, relationships, and hearts...and He can perform miracles we never dreamed of. I don't pretend to know what moves the hand of God, but I believe we live in His favor only when we are devoted to Him and do our best to live upright lives. Give your all to God and watch Him do impossible things in your life.

John 3:16 (The Message)

This is how much God loved the world: He gave His Son, His one and only Son. And this is why: so that no one need be destroyed; by believing in Him, anyone can have a whole and lasting life.

Whatever version of the Bible one may read, the marvelous message of John 3:16 is clear: God loves us. He loves each of us so much that He sent Jesus to the earth to show us how to live and to bear the punishment we deserve. This message is not for a select few, for God has no favorites. The Good News is for anyone who will believe. The reward for believing in Jesus cannot be described or measured. Who can put a value on whole, abundant life? How much are eternal joy and everlasting peace worth? These priceless treasures are gifts--gifts God gives to all who choose to be His own. Don't let anyone or anything keep you from experiencing the amazing life your Lord and King made possible through the gift of Jesus Christ, His Son.

Isaiah 30:18

Yet the Lord longs to be gracious to you; He rises to show you compassion. For the Lord is a God of justice. Blessed are all who wait for Him!

In the verses before this, God was recounting the sins of an obstinate, rebellious people and stating the inevitable results of their refusal to repent. They were deceitful and unwilling to listen. They rejected His message and heaped sin upon sin. They looked to Pharaoh's help rather than God's. They deserved to be deserted by God and punished for their sins. But there's this amazing word: "Yet." Even after all they had done--after all we do--God still longs to be gracious. He still wants to show us compassion. He still wants to forgive us and to bless us. His compassion and forgiveness are there waiting for us whenever we turn to Him. Regardless of what we have done in the past, there is a "yet" for us, too. Rejoice in your second…third…ten millionth chance at a blessed abundant life.

1 John 2:1,2

My dear children, I write this to you so that you will not sin. But if anybody does sin, we have one who speaks to the Father in our defense--Jesus Christ, the Righteous One. He is the atoning sacrifice for our sins, and not only for ours but also for the sins of the whole world.

Some people think that Christians should never stumble, never make a mistake, and never sin. Ideally, that is right. We should pray that we are always able to live how God wants us to live. Realistically speaking, no matter how much we love Him and try to lead perfect lives, we will still mess up. I love these verses because they remind me that even when I fail, Jesus is pleading my case. "Yes, she messed up again," I think He says, "but she is mine. I already paid the debt she owes. I have redeemed her."

And then God smiles and says, "Yes, you have. Her slate is clean." Just in case it slipped your mind, He does the same for you!

Romans 11:11a

Again I ask: Did they stumble so as to fall beyond recovery? Not at all!

Paul was speaking here of the Israelites, God's chosen people. They had rejected His Word, bowed to idols, and killed His prophets and His son; yet there was still hope for them. God simply does not give up on His children. I have known people who think God can't forgive them. Some think that even if He does save them, He will not really love them the same way He loves His obedient children. Well, here's a news flash. There are no obedient children. We have all tripped, slipped, stumbled, plunged headlong--even taken a flying leap into total disobedience, and He loves us still. Jesus came to earth and bore the punishment for our sins in a cruel death. He did that willingly because He knew we could not be obedient children, and He wants us to spend eternity with Him. Never hang your head remembering past sins; lift your eyes to Heaven and thank Him for washing them away.

Psalm 103:17,18

But from everlasting to everlasting the Lord's love is with those who fear (respect, honor) him, and his righteousness with their children's children—with those who keep his covenant and remember to obey his precepts.

One of the things about God that brings me the most comfort is His steadfastness. His love for us is unconditional...period. It isn't just when we are behaving ourselves, out doing good works, or on our face in prayer. He loves us always. Not only that, He will love our children and our children's children! I thank God that there were people in my life who feared God and helped me along the way. I thank Him for the prayers of the ancestors I never knew, for I believe they kept me from many dangers. Even if you don't have a rich heritage of family who loved God, you can leave a rich legacy for your children, grandchildren, and others God has placed in your life. Honor God with your life and be obedient. Doing so will bless you, and it will bless those whose lives you touch now and for generations to come.

Matthew 5: 23,24

Therefore, if you are offering your gift at the altar and there remember that your brother has something against you, leave your gift there in front of the altar. First go and be reconciled to your brother; then come and offer your gift.

It is crucial to our walk to seek forgiveness when we have wronged someone else. This passage tells us we should not even bring a gift to the altar if there is something unresolved between us and a brother or sister--another Christian. These offenses don't have to be intentional. There are times when we may hurt another without meaning to...or even times when we don't think we have wronged someone at all. The fact is God wants

His children to get along with each other. Who is to blame is not the important thing. Healing the hurt and moving on in harmony is. When we apologize to a Christian brother or sister, even if we don't think we are wrong, this is an act of obedience. It pleases God and demonstrates that we are serious about showing love to one another. If you have unresolved problems with your fellow Christians, I pray that you will be able to make things right soon.

Galatians 4:4-7

But when the time had fully come, God sent his Son, born of a woman, born under law, to redeem those under law, that we might receive the full rights of sons. Because you are sons, God sent the Spirit of his Son into our hearts, the Spirit who calls out, "Abba, Father." So you are no longer a slave but a son; and since you are a son, God has made you also an heir.

Many people are involved in genealogy. They work long and hard to prove who their ancestors were and are thrilled if they find that somehow they are related to George Washington. But we don't have to trace our family tree where God is concerned. He has no grandchildren or great-grandchildren. We are His children. Period. He has accepted us into His family, and we have received full rights as sons and daughters of the Almighty. We are joint heirs with Jesus! Our inheritance, which is greater than we can ever think or imagine, can never perish, spoil, or fade and is kept for us in Heaven. (Remember 1 Peter 1:4?) He has even sent the Holy Spirit to live within us and remind us of our secure and priceless place in His heart. May God's peace be upon you today, Precious Child of God.

Proverbs 24:24,25

Whoever says to the guilty, "You are innocent"—peoples will curse him and nations denounce him. But it will go well with those who convict the guilty, and rich blessing will come upon them.

It is popular these days to accept a live-and-let-live philosophy. Many believe that what others do is their business, and we should mind our own. I am not advocating examining everybody else's life and pronouncing him or her guilty. We should, however, know enough about what God says in His Word to recognize sin when we see it. What we cannot do is give our approval to actions that we know are against God's unchanging decrees. To do that confuses those who don't know God's laws and may lead them farther away from Him. Our main focus in life should be bringing God glory and bringing others to Him. We can't be wishy-washy about our faith and act as though there is no divine law. There is, and God expects us to know it, show it, and live under it.

Jonah 2:2

He said, "In my distress I called to the Lord, and He answered me."

A few days ago, our electricity flickered. That is never good news. Usually, as was the case this time, some fuses on our cable will blow, and we will be without television and internet. We called the company and, since it was a holiday, we got a recording with the assurance that they would fix our problem as soon as possible. That happened to be twenty-four hours later. I am so glad that God doesn't operate like the cable company. I'm grateful that I will never get a recording when I call to Him. I am happy He doesn't take vacation days. I'm thankful that I don't have to wait until He has helped someone else before He helps me. God is always on duty. He is always watching over me; He is always listening for my cry. I am at the top of His list--and guess what. You are, too! Our God is so great and His heart is so big that each of us has a special place. Don't wait until you need His help to call out to Him. Visit with Him today and thank Him for His constant and unfailing love.

John 15:5

(Jesus speaking) I am the vine; you are the branches. If a man remains in me and I in him, he will bear much fruit; apart from me you can do nothing.

Imagine branches lying on the ground connected to nothing. Never mind how much fruit they will produce; how long will they survive? With this analogy, Jesus gives us a true picture of our lives. Without Him, we will wither and die, having experienced no joy and having produced nothing worthwhile. Unlike actual vines, we choose whether we remain connected. We can also choose to be grafted back in if we leave--but why leave? Jesus is the source of every good thing in our lives. Nothing of real value comes unless it comes through Him. Through Him flow joy, peace, hope, love, and mercy. Through Him flow courage, strength, and a reason for living. Diligently guard your connection to your Lord so that you will be nourished and sustained by Him.

2 Timothy 3:16 (The Message)

Every part of Scripture is God-breathed and useful one way or another--showing us the truth, exposing our rebellion, correcting our mistakes, training us to live God's way.

Have you ever tried to assemble something without following the instructions? This piece might go here...maybe this will fit there.... Sometimes, we can be successful that way. More often we can't. There is a piece left over, something we forgot to consider. The finished product may look complete, and it may even work for a time...but it won't work properly, and it won't hold up. The best plan for us is just start over and do it right. Our lives, too, are meant to be assembled following God's instructions. We will never be successful on our own. We can't guess what His will is. We can't rearrange or leave out what He has told us and expect our lives to work smoothly. Because of His mercy and goodness, though, we can start over. It's never too late to lay the disassembled pieces of our lives before Him. Don't try to build your life by some "gospel according to you." Let God show you in His Word. Building your life according to His instructions is the only way to live a successful, happy, peaceful, fulfilled life.

Jeremiah 10:24

Correct me, Lord, but only with justice--not in your anger, lest you reduce me to nothing.

No matter how far we walk in our Christian lives, there are times when we mess up. We do or say something we shouldn't, or we don't do or say something we should. If we are serious about our walk with Christ, we know that everything that may come between God and us should be rooted out. We need correction, but...we would like for it to be as painless as possible. We could say, "I want you to show me where I am wrong, God, but be easy on me when you do...and please don't do it if you're angry with me." And whether we have prayed this prayer or not, this is exactly how God treats us. He will make us very aware of things that don't please Him, but He does it with love. Tenderly, kindly, and patiently, He shapes and molds us as long as we are willing. As Almighty God, He has the power to destroy us with a word; as our Heavenly Father, He loves us enough not to. How wonderful is that?

Psalm 119:105 KJV

Thy Word is a lamp unto my feet, and a light unto my path.

Have you ever been in complete darkness? I remember taking a tour through a cavern when the guides turned off all lights to let us experience total blackness. I felt off-balance; I was completely disoriented. I was afraid to move for fear that I could fall into some abyss. When we try to travel through life without God's light, we are in much more danger than we could ever be in a cavern. There are deadly pitfalls waiting at every turn, disguised and indiscernible to mere mortals. God's Word shows us these pitfalls. It shows us how to live fulfilling lives. It warns, encourages, and comforts us. It teaches us about Christ, who came as the Light. The Bible doesn't work just sitting on the table or being carried to church. It fills your life with light and hope when you open the pages and allow it to fill your mind and your heart.

Psalm 37:23,24

If the Lord delights in a man's way, He makes his steps firm; though he stumble, he will not fall, for the Lord upholds him with His hand.

Our path through this world is littered with mistakes. One of the wonderful things about God is that we don't have to walk a perfect path to please Him. We bring Him joy by trying--sincerely wanting to follow in Christ's footsteps. When we stumble (notice it doesn't say 'if'), God Himself holds us up and keeps us from falling. How great is that? Our failures do not sentence us to permanent separation from God. He doesn't sit in Heaven and shake His head in disgust. He doesn't say, "Well, that's that. I'm through. No more chances." No, He gently reaches down, catches us, and puts us back on the right path. "Try again, Child," He says. "You can do this." And you know what? With His help, we can!

Matthew 18:21,22

Then Peter came to Jesus and asked, "Lord, how many times shall I forgive my brother when he sins against me? Up to seven times?" Jesus answered, "I tell you, not seven times, but seventy times seven."

I remember when as a child I heard the parable of the unmerciful servant for the first time. I was practicing my math, I guess, as I asked my mother a question that was bothering me. "Does Jesus really mean we have to forgive someone 490 times?" I couldn't imagine that was right. Once seemed generous to me.

I remember her answer: "I think Jesus picked a big number because it would be hard for us to keep track that long. You are always supposed to forgive." At the time, I didn't like that answer. Surely there was a "get even" time. I have grown to love that answer because I know that's how God forgives me...always. He won't run out of second chances for me... or for you. How wonderful! Today is a new day. Make the most of your new chance.

Joshua 24:15b

But as for me and my house, we will serve the Lord.

Joshua is one of my favorite people in the Bible. He was strong and courageous, a mighty warrior who believed nothing was impossible with God on his side. He was also determined that he, as well as all those in his house, would serve the Lord. Some may think we are responsible only for our own actions, and in some ways this is true. But we do have the responsibility to do everything we can to help those we know come to God. Admonish, encourage, love, and pray diligently for all those in your circle of influence. Never give up. Be like Joshua. Determine to stand firm and fight for the lives and souls those you love.

Genesis 19:26

But Lot's wife looked back, and she became a pillar of salt.

The account of Lot's wife puzzled me when I was young. It seemed like such a natural thing for her to do--to look back when burning sulfur was raining down on Sodom and Gomorrah. I would have wanted to see what all the commotion was behind me, too! I understood she disobeyed. But why did God care if she looked back? What was the significance? It may have showed her reluctance to leave. She had been living in a godless place, and God had rescued her. In spite of that, she lagged behind, perhaps yearning for parts of her old life. God has rescued us from godless places, too--times when we were far from Him. When He reaches down to rescue us from a place we never should have been and sets us back on the way that we should go, we should not waste precious time. Looking back can paralyze us in our journey and keep us from reaching the heights God has planned for us. We should thank Him for His amazing grace that set us free and move on.

Galatians 6:9

Let us not become weary in doing good, for at the proper time we will reap a harvest if we do not give up.

We like to see results. We tend to expect everything we do to produce results, and we prefer them to be immediate. It's hard for us to get it through our thick skulls that God is never in a hurry. He has His own timetable, and it doesn't match ours. Everything we do for God accomplishes something--somewhere, sometime. He has a harvest time for us if we do not give up. We must keep on doing good, loving and helping others, whether our actions seem to be having any effect or not. Don't give up. Don't be discouraged. Nothing we do for God goes unnoticed or unrewarded by the One who gives us life itself.

Jude 1:24

To Him who is able to keep you from falling and to present you before His glorious presence without fault and with great joy--to the only God our Savior be glory, majesty, power and authority, through Jesus Christ our Lord, before all ages, now and forevermore! Amen.

Every person on earth will stand before God some day whether he or she believes it or not. Many who do believe it don't like to think about it, but as Christians, we should look forward to that day without fear. Christ can keep us from falling, and He is willing to present us...to claim us as His own! We will come before the throne of God without fault because Christ has taken our guilt away. I like to imagine Jesus smiling as He takes my hand and leads me to God's throne. "She is one of mine," He will say. Then words, even "great joy," cannot begin to express how I will feel. I hope you, too, are confident of this promise. It is for all of us, you know.

Psalm 38:4,18

My guilt has overwhelmed me like a burden too heavy to bear...I confess my iniquity; I am troubled by my sin.

David was miserable when he wrote this. He was overwhelmed with guilt, trying to carry a burden he could not. David's future, however, was not bleak because he recognized his sin and the devastating effect it was having on his life. He also knew what to do about it: he petitioned God and confessed his sin to Him. God is always ready to forgive us and to carry our burdens for us, but there is something we must do. We have to admit we are wrong and be truly remorseful. These verses should not cause us to feel sadness and despair. They should give us hope and joy. We never have to be overwhelmed by guilt, for God has made a way for us to be forgiven and redeemed, cleansed of our sins and filled with His peace.

Romans 3:22,23

This righteousness from God comes through faith in Jesus Christ to all who believe. There is no difference, for all have sinned and fall short of the glory of God.

There is one thing we have in common. We have all sinned. It is useless and senseless to try to measure ourselves against another, somehow believing that we are less guilty if we can declare another more guilty. Sin is sin. It doesn't have to be some great, obvious infraction of God's or man's law. Many sins are secret, sometimes existing only in the mind and heart. Sin is missing the mark set for us...breaking God's Law... being estranged from our Lord. It is the failure to be what we ought to be. All of us are guilty, yet because of God's great mercy, we can be washed clean through faith in Christ. Never think that there is too much in the past for God to forgive, for there isn't.

Proverbs 4:20-22

My son, pay attention to what I say; listen closely to my words. Do not let them out of your sight, keep them within your heart; for they are life to those who find them and health to a man's whole body.

God tells us many times that we should meditate on His Word. It is so important to our health and well-being that He reminds us over and over. We are to give full attention to what He says and meditate on it day and night. Some people may learn the books of the Bible, the history of the Jewish people, and be able to quote John 3:16 and a dozen other verses. That's good, but it is not enough. We are supposed to keep His Word in the midst of our hearts! Just look at what He promises us if we give attention to His words--life and health. There is a strong connection between the thoughts in our minds and the health of our bodies. God says so. If we meditate on His words and keep them in the center of our hearts, we will benefit physically. Stress, worry, anxiety, fear--all that stuff that messes with our heads and then attacks our bodies--these will leave when we fill ourselves with the Word of God. Pick a verse today and repeat it over and over. Think about what it means to your life and have a carefree day, ready for anything.

John 17:20,21

My prayer is not for them (the disciples) alone. I pray also for those who will believe in me through their message, that all of them may be one, Father, just as you are in me and I am in you. May they also be in us so that the world may believe that you have sent me.

It amazes me to think that Jesus actually prayed for me...and for you. We are those who believe because of the message, the Good News, that the followers of Jesus have spread abroad. The Bible tells us that God knew us before He laid the foundations of the world, and when Jesus prayed just before His arrest, we--you and I--were in His mind. It should be significant that at this critical time, Jesus chose to pray that we would be one with each other...forgiving, encouraging, helping, and caring for each other. Jesus gave His life, His all. How much of ourselves are we willing to give?

Mark 14:30,31

"I tell you the truth," Jesus answered, "today—yes, tonight—before the rooster crows twice you yourself will disown me three times."

But Peter insisted emphatically, "Even if I have to die with you, I will never disown you." And all the others said the same.

Of course, we know that Peter did just as Jesus predicted. All of the disciples deserted Him following His arrest. We probably don't understand why Peter, so determined to be faithful, failed so quickly. But then again, we don't understand why we fail either, but we do. This account should be a comfort to us, though, because even though Peter denied Christ and deserted Him, Christ didn't deny or desert Peter. Peter failed at a critical time, but Jesus still loved him, forgave him, and used him to help spread the Gospel anyway. Peter was truly remorseful, and it was as though he had never denied Christ at all. It's the same for us. When we are sincerely sorry for our failures, Christ forgives us; it's as though we hadn't sinned at all. That's why He went to the cross--to take the punishment for our sins so we don't have to. Our slate is clean because of the blood shed by our Precious Savior. Praise be to God for His amazing grace.

Luke 22:32b

And when you have turned back....

Jesus knew Peter was going to deny Him three times, yet He made this simple statement: "And when you have turned back...." There is no suggestion here of a long period of time for Peter to pay for his actions before he could come back...no hint of great deeds of sacrifice that he must perform. True, Peter was crushed and broken-hearted, but this was not something that Jesus placed on him. Rather, it was the natural outcome of realizing that he had betrayed his Lord. All Peter had to do was turn back. It was up to him when that would be. It is the same for us. When we betray Jesus, it is up to us how long we stay away. He is always ready, willing, and hoping for us to come back quickly. Never think that returning to Him is more complicated than that. Just come back to His welcoming arms.

Psalm 143:8

Let the morning bring me word of your unfailing love, for I have put my trust in you. Show me the way I should go, for to you I lift up my soul.

When we set out on a trip, we usually program our GPS. Often, we don't stick to the original planned route, and the GPS will begin to chirp, "Recalculating. Recalculating." Soon it has an alternate plan to get us to our destination although it may not be as direct as the original one. God has a perfect plan for our lives—a way that will lead us through with the fewest obstacles and with the greatest peace and happiness. When we wander off and leave the path He has chosen for us, though, God doesn't throw up His hands and give up on us. He chooses an alternate route that will still lead us to our destination even though it will be harder than the route He mapped out in the first place. No matter how many detours we take, there is still a way to perfect eternal peace with Him because of His unfailing love for each of us. Ask Him today and every day: "Lord, show me the way I should go." Then obey Him.

Acts 1:9-11

After He said this, He was taken up before their very eyes, and a cloud hid Him from their sight. They were looking intently up into the sky as He was going, when suddenly two men dressed in white stood beside them. "Men of Galilee," they said, "why do you stand here looking into the sky? This same Jesus, who has been taken from you into heaven, will come back in the same way you have seen Him go into heaven."

The Lord was leaving in the clouds, and the angels asked a strange question. Surely they didn't expect the disciples to say, "Okay, there Jesus goes. We're done here." There's not a person with eyes anywhere who would not have watched Him go up into the clouds. Tragically, however, there are millions who are not watching for Him to come back. Jesus said He would return, plain and simple. Christians argue about when this will take place, but no one really knows. That doesn't mean we shouldn't be waiting and watching, even yearning for the day He returns. Remember what Paul told Timothy? There is a crown of righteousness, which the Lord will award to those who yearn for His appearing. Whether He is coming to call up the church or coming to take each of us home in death, be ready and wait expectantly for Him. The King of Kings is coming.

Genesis 25:30-33

He (Esau) said to Jacob, "Quick, let me have some of that red stew! I am famished!" (That is why he was also called Edom).

Jacob replied, "First sell me your birthright."

"Look, I am about to die," Esau said. "What good is the birthright to me?"

But Jacob said "Swear to me first." So he swore an oath to him, selling his birthright to Jacob.

Esau was hungry. He was willing to give up something of great value for immediate gratification. He was living in the present, showing a disregard for the future blessings of his birthright. Without a vision for the future, he chose to satisfy his wants at the moment. We are like Esau when we base our actions and make our choices on what we want now rather than the promises of God for our future. Never risk losing the joy of tomorrow. God's greatest blessings in life will come to us when we are willing to trust Him and wait.

Genesis 26:1-3a, 6

Now there was a famine in the land—besides the earlier famine of Abraham's time—and Isaac went to Abimelech king of the Philistines in Gerar. The Lord appeared to Isaac and said, "Do not go down to Egypt; live in the land where I tell you to live. Stay in this land for a while, and I will be with you and bless you."… So Isaac stayed in Gerar.

Isaac was facing a famine. It may have seemed logical to leave his situation and go to Egypt, but God told him to stay. If you read farther in this account, you find that Isaac planted crops and reaped one hundred fold; his herds and flocks increased until he became very wealthy. God blessed him because he trusted and obeyed God regardless of how things appeared. What about us? We don't have to be delivered from every hardship to be blessed, either. A great blessing comes to us when we are faithful <u>through</u> our troubles. Don't be discouraged if you are in a time of famine. God can change your circumstances in an instant, and He can carry you safely through. Just lift up your eyes to Him, obey what He is placing on your heart, and wait for the end of your famine.

Colossians 3:23,24

Whatever you do, work at it with all your heart, as working for the Lord, not for men, since you know that you will receive an inheritance from the Lord as a reward. It is the Lord Christ you are serving.

We all know what ingratitude feels like. Maybe we've experienced it in dealing with a boss, a friend, or our families. We went out of our way, "busted" ourselves, and our efforts weren't even acknowledged, much less appreciated. When we feel this way, we are not considering this important fact: we are here to serve God, not men. He wants us to do the very best we can in whatever we do. Make this day between you and God. Serve Him with your whole heart, knowing that the only reward that really matters is living so He says, "Well done."

Romans 6:23

For the wages of sin is death, but the gift of God is eternal life in Christ Jesus our Lord.

We all at times have wished that there were no consequences for sin in our lives. Unfortunately, there are. Sin can cause the death of relationships. It can kill our health and our hope. It can even cause eternal separation from God. Whenever we violate His laws, we set some force in motion that could destroy us if it were not for the mercy of God. Unrepented sin will grow, and we will reap a harvest we do not want. However, whenever we confess our sins to Him and turn away from them, He is faithful to forgive us. Many of the seeds of disaster we have planted may never sprout, and because of His great mercy, we won't receive the wages we have earned. Instead, God gives us eternal life, a gift of love already bought by Jesus' sacrifice on the Cross.

Luke 23:34a

Jesus said, "Father, forgive them, for they do not know what they are doing."

Sometimes in life we have to deal with people whose whole mission seems to be hurting someone else. We may try to understand why they act the way they do or say the things they say, but the only way to explain it is to realize that they don't know Jesus. They are deluded and deceived...and they don't know what they are doing. This is true for all mean-spirited, spiteful people. They don't realize they are being used by Satan and serving the father of all liars. They don't understand that the misery they heap upon another will multiply when it comes back to them. They don't know that they are grieving the King of Kings by hurting one of His precious children. What a dangerous thing to do! Forgiving is not impossible when you consider that they don't have a clue about the only thing that matters in this world--pleasing our Savior. When others hurt you or someone you care about, just hand the problem to Jesus and let go. Don't let anyone who doesn't even know what he is doing steal your joy.

John 12:21

They (some Greeks) came to Philip, who was from Bethsaida in Galilee, with a request. "Sir," they said, "we would like to see Jesus."

Isn't it wonderful that we don't have to get permission from someone else to see Jesus? We can see Him in the beauty of nature all around us. We can see Him in the helping hands of a friend. We can see Him in the eyes of an aged one devoted to Him. We can see Him in the face of a laughing child. We can see Him through the encouraging, consoling words of one who cares. He surrounds us with His love and His amazing grace, and He fills us with joy, contentment, and peace. We can see Him every day in many ways, and we what see with our hearts is more beautiful than anything we could ever see with our eyes.

Zechariah 4:10a

Who despises the day of small things? Men will rejoice when they see the plumb line in the hand of Zerubbabel.

God gave Zerubbabel the privilege of rebuilding the Temple. It was a task of immense proportions, yet it had to begin with something very small. The men rejoiced because they had faith and a vision of what could be. Each thing that we are able to accomplish on this earth for our King begins with something small. Never think that what you are doing is insignificant, for everything we do for Him helps someone, somehow, somewhere, some time. God can take a spark of a dream, and with a ray of hope and a grain of faith, He can turn it into something wonderful.

Psalm 71:14,15

But as for me, I will always have hope; I praise you more and more. My mouth will tell of your righteousness, of your salvation all day long, though I know not its measure.

Hope is a great blessing from God. It is what carries us through the heartaches and tragedies of life and makes us able to face the future with confidence. However, holding on to hope is a choice. Every day, people encounter nearly identical storms as others, yet some sail through and others are submerged in a sea of despair. The difference is Christ, the foundation of our hope, the Omnipotent King of the Universe who loved us each enough to die for us. As Christians, our lives should be filled with hope, which is strengthened as we offer praise and testimony of God's greatness. My prayer is that you have a wonderful day, filled with hope and the joy of trusting your Lord. As for me, I choose to!

Luke 15:21

The son said to him, "Father, I have sinned against heaven and against you. I am no longer worthy to be called your son."

Have you ever felt unworthy? Who hasn't. As the prodigal son did, we have left the safety and security of our Father's fold and wandered off--maybe to a foreign land, squandering the things of the most value to us. We may think that it's impossible to come back and that we are unworthy to be called children of God. But--wait a minute. Who determines our value? Does Satan? Do the people around us? Do we? No, God Almighty does, and He already determined how much we are worth. He thought we were worth coming to earth and taking the punishment for all the sins we have ever committed. He thought we were worth dying for. Never feel unworthy. You are God's treasure, forgiven, redeemed, and loved unconditionally by the One who created you.

2 Timothy 2:4 NKJV

No one engaged in warfare entangles himself with the affairs of this life, that he may please he who enlisted him as a soldier.

We are soldiers in God's army. Our enemy is Satan, and his mission is to destroy our witness, our families, our faith, and our lives. Luring us into becoming entangled with the affairs of this life is his greatest weapon. He tries to busy us with everyday nothing, leaving little time for God. He tries to convince us that what we want or what is convenient for us should determine what we do. Our mission is to live lives pleasing to God, showing Christ to the world and helping our fellow human beings along the way. It is our duty as soldiers to put this mission before anything else, for though we are in the world, we are not of the world. May your day be productive and pleasing to God, free from entanglements that accomplish no good thing.

Hebrews 2:1

We must pay more careful attention, therefore, to what we have heard, so that we do not drift away.

Picture, if you will, a boat tied to a pier in a calm, protected cove. As long as the boat remains at the pier, it will not drift into deep, rough waters. It won't be floating aimlessly, heading who knows where. We are like this boat, and God is like the pier. Our obedience and our diligence in study and prayer make up an indestructible rope that ties us to the pier and holds us fast. If we sever our rope and drift away, we can choose to return. There can, however, be damage to our lives--long lasting damage--if we allow ourselves to go off into uncharted waters. Staying tied to the pier doesn't just happen. Resolve today to keep the knot in your rope secure. Study His Word, spend time in prayer, and stay close to the pier--your God and King.

Romans 13:8

Let no debt remain outstanding, except the continuing debt to love one another, for he who loves his fellowman has fulfilled the law.

Debt is a part of life. Most of us, at one time or another, have owed money to someone else because we purchased something we did or didn't need. When we finished paying off the debt, it was a time for rejoicing. The Bible teaches us to be faithful in paying our debts, but there is one debt we can never finish paying. We owe love to one another. We owe each other compassion, kindness, and concern. No matter what we did for others on Monday, when we wake up on Tuesday, we owe them again. When we love each other, we fulfill the law. No burnt offerings, no great sacrifices, and no endless rituals are needed to earn God's approval. God's unconditional, constant, eternal love for us is our example. Work on the debt you owe by letting His love shine on others through you...daily, without ceasing.

Ecclesiastes 12:13

Now all has been heard; here is the conclusion of the matter: Fear God and keep his commandments, for this is the whole duty of man.

Living a Christian life is not complicated. God doesn't ask us to do things we can't do or give us tasks we can't understand. If His Word has told us to do something or not to do something, it is possible for us to obey. That doesn't mean we will never slip or even fall flat in our walk. We will, but only when we have chosen to disobey. God knew every sin we would commit before He created us, and He still created us. He also made a way for our sins to be forgiven by sending the perfect, sinless Lamb to take the punishment for us. He doesn't ask much of us: to respect, honor, and love Him, and to live as He teaches us. He even sent the Holy Spirit to help us! All we have to do is be willing to give Him control; He will do the rest.

Psalm 45:7

You love righteousness and hate wickedness; therefore God, your God, has set you above your companions by anointing you with the oil of joy.

People strive to be happy. They set goals and make plans in an attempt to get something or do something that they think will bring them happiness. Even if they are successful, this happiness is only temporary. Tomorrow or the next day they will have to come up with another goal or another plan. Joy, on the other hand, is not something a person can attain on his or her own. Joy is a gift from God--an inner contentment that comes from being at peace with oneself. God chooses to bless our lives with joy when we try to live our lives to please Him, and I believe that the depth of our joy depends upon the extent of our dedication. I pray that today you dedicate yourself more fully to Him and feel the precious anointing of His joy in your life.

Acts 3:16

By faith in the name of Jesus, this man whom you see and know was made strong. It is Jesus' name and the faith that comes through Him that has given this complete healing to Him, as you can all see.

Peter spoke these words after the crippled beggar was healed. Often people concentrate on physical healing, and it is a miraculous thing. But I can safely say, without a doubt, that physical healing is not the greatest gift of healing Christ is willing to give us. Much greater is the gift of spiritual healing, the gift of being able to put behind us the past with all its disappointments, pain, and failures and walk in the newness of life He promised. The man in this account was completely healed by faith in the name of Jesus. That is where our complete healing lies, too.

1 Samuel 12:23

As for me, far be it from me that I should sin against the Lord by failing to pray for you.

Do we take our responsibility to pray for each other seriously enough? Samuel considered failing to pray a sin against God. Even though we don't hold a position equal to Samuel as judge over a whole nation, we are told over and over in the New Testament to pray for each other. Remember James 5:16? Our fervent prayers can accomplish a great deal. Prayer brings us into the very presence of God. It builds us up and fills us with contentment found no other way. It also moves His hands, changing circumstances, lives, and hearts. Give an incomparable gift to others and to yourself. Spend time in prayer.

John 21:4-7

Early in the morning, Jesus stood on the shore, but the disciples did not realize that it was Jesus. He called out to them, "Friends, haven't you any fish?"

"No," they answered.

He said, "Throw your net on the right side of the boat and you will find some."

When they did, they were unable to haul the net in because of the large number of fish. Then the disciple whom Jesus loved said to Peter, "It is the Lord!" As soon as Simon Peter heard him say, "It is the Lord," he wrapped his outer garment around him (for he had taken it off) and jumped into the water.

"Impetuous" describes Peter well. He was passionate and impulsive, quick to act in a big way. And here, not being willing to wait an extra minute, he jumped out of the boat. The boat was the safe way to get to shore, but Peter was so eager to be close to Jesus that he just jumped. The other disciples got there, but they missed some precious time in the presence of the Master. Even today, there are times when we have to leave the safety of our boat and jump into unfamiliar waters. If, like Peter, we are sure that it is the Lord's voice we hear, we should act without hesitation. Every second we spend closer to Him is worth whatever effort it takes--even if, especially if, we have to jump out of the boat.

Romans 11:23

And if they do not persist in unbelief, they will be grafted in, for God is able to graft them in again.

In this passage of Scripture, Paul compares God's chosen people to an olive tree. He explains how the Jewish people were cut off because of their unbelief, and the Gentiles were grafted in and accepted into God's family. The important point here is that those who were cut off still have the chance to come back. Though they were once cast off and separated by their own choice, God is able to graft them in again. This is a beautiful example of God's great love for us: even a branch once headed for the refuse pile of life can bloom and flourish again through the mercy and power of God.

Psalm 119:32

I run in the path of your commands, for you have set my heart free.

Do you ever get weary? You know--feeling bogged down, done in, worn out, and used up? Sometimes we just trudge along, allowing too much world to deplete our energy...and our joy. Being physically tired is one thing, but there is an easy cure for weariness of heart. It is found in obeying God. He alone can erase bitterness, hurt, and the pain of guilt. He alone can set our hearts free from the bonds of disobedience and regret. Don't spend another minute stumbling around on a path to nowhere. Get on the path God has laid out for you...and run with a free heart.

1 Thessalonians 5:16

Be joyful always.

I used to think that when I was unhappy, it was someone else's fault. They did or said something or didn't do or say something that messed up my day. Now I know that joy is a choice. We choose how we will react to people and events around us, and therefore we choose whether or not they can rob us of our joy. The word "joyful" actually means "experiencing, causing, or showing joy." Most people concentrate on the first part--experiencing joy; however, we cannot be joyful ourselves without making a conscious effort to cause joy and to show joy, too. What if each one of us determined to show joy in all circumstances and cause joy wherever we could? Then the first part of the definition would also be true. We would experience great joy--the joy that Jesus gave His life to give us.

John 6:35

Then Jesus declared, "I am the bread of life. He who comes to me will never go hungry, and he who believes in me will never be thirsty."

Food is an undeniable necessity. We know that it is required for our survival, and we spend whatever time, money, and effort it takes to be sure that we are physically fed. We are usually more concerned with taking care of the part of us that will die than nourishing the part of us that will live on. We sometimes put up with depression, worry, unhappiness, and problems too big for us to handle, never considering that the solution to each of these can be found in Christ. Jesus is willing and able to take away all hunger, all thirst, and all emptiness. Don't neglect the Source of everything good; let Him feed you, fill you, and nourish you to fullness of life.

Hebrews 11:13a

All these people were still living by faith when they died. They did not receive the things promised; they only saw them and welcomed them from a distance.

The verses before this were speaking of some of the great men of faith: Abel, Enoch, Noah, and Abraham. The things God had promised them were slow in coming, but they continued to believe. We must follow their example when we are waiting for the hands of God to move. A thousand years is as a day to Him, and the answers we want this afternoon may not come for years. We should be diligent in our prayers for concerns of the present, but we should also be praying for the future that we know we will not see, for our descendants and the world they will live in. God hears our prayers, and He is never late. Have faith that your answers are coming whether you will see them or not.

2 Kings 20:2-5a

Hezekiah turned his face to the wall and prayed to the Lord, "Remember, O Lord, how I have walked before you faithfully and with wholehearted devotion and have done what is good in your eyes." And Hezekiah wept bitterly.

Before Isaiah had left the middle court, the word of the Lord came to him: "Go back and tell Hezekiah, the leader of my people, 'This is what the Lord, the God of your father David, says: I have heard your prayer and seen your tears; I will heal you.'"

Hezekiah was at the point of death--as sick as he could get. God Himself had said he would not recover. Hezekiah asked God to remember the things he (Hezekiah) had done to serve God faithfully, and God granted the plea from Hezekiah's heart and healed him. We could debate forever what moved the hand of God here. What we can be sure of is that we should never give up on ourselves or someone else we care about, however hopeless the situation seems to those around us. Our Heavenly Father hears our prayers and sees our tears--and He loves us deeply. There's always a chance that an Isaiah is coming our way with good news.

John 1:12,13

Yet to all who received Him, to those who believed in His name, He gave the right to become children of God—children born not of natural descent, nor of human decision or a husband's will, but born of God.

Child of God. I think sometimes we become so accustomed to these words that we forget the incredible immenseness of their meaning. Here we are, invisible specks on a planet that is itself an invisible speck in the grandeur of God's creation. There are billions of us who follow thousands of years of others who have lived on this earth...yet God loves each of us and singles each of us out to give us the right to be called His child. One would think we would have to do some heroic, gargantuan deed to earn such a priceless treasure. Yet, all we have to do is believe in Him and receive Him into our lives and hearts. This inheritance that comes from God is a gift--unearned, undeserved, and incomprehensible. I pray that your heart swells with joy when you contemplate your place in the heart of God Almighty.

Job 38:4a

Where were you when I laid the earth's foundation?

I can't say I understand much about the miracle of earth. I don't see how it remains in orbit, circling the sun while suspended in space. It amazes me to consider how it stays the exact distance from the sun, creating the perfect climate for all God's creation and producing everything needed to sustain all life. I can't explain even the smallest of the miracles of nature. Much less am I able to fathom its grandeur and complexity. I do know one thing, though. I know where I was when God laid the earth's foundation. I was in His mind and in His heart...and so were you.

Psalm 143:8

Let the morning bring me word of your unfailing love, for I have put my trust in you. Show me the way I should go, for to you I lift up my soul.

Sometimes we human beings wear down. We are tired--physically, mentally, emotionally, and perhaps spiritually. Maybe there is a good reason. Maybe there is not. It is interesting that David asks for relief in the morning. He seems to know that the darkness must persist for its allotted time. When it is over, in the morning, David wants to be reminded again of God's great love, and he wants guidance from the Almighty. Whenever you face a night, a time of darkness in your life, lift up your soul to God and trust Him. There will be a morning, and you will see His unfailing love work in your life.

Psalm 127:1

Unless the Lord builds the house, its builders labor in vain. Unless the Lord watches over the city, the watchmen stand guard in vain.

There are millions of people who think they are living independently of God. They credit their own cleverness for all their successes and depend upon their own ingenuity for their future. It is sad that they don't realize everything we have comes from God--all our material blessings, our health, and our true joy. Even sadder is the fact that many people don't accept the fact that God's hand has built and sustained this nation, and they want to put Him in a tiny box to be opened only on Sunday mornings in a private church, out of the view and minds of all but a few. Our families, homes, and lives are safe only through God's watchful care. So is this nation. Pray for a return to the faith that made our country strong.

Job 34:33

Should God then reward you on your terms when you refuse to repent? You must decide, not I; so tell me what you know. (Elihu speaking to Job)

This question should cause us all to pause and think. Do our actions keep us from getting answers from God? Should we expect Him to rescue us time after time and protect us day after day if we are unwilling to obey Him? We must decide this for ourselves, but that doesn't mean that there is more than one correct answer. We must be constant in our efforts to obey; we must be diligent in repenting when we fail. Only through obedience and repentance can we expect to receive the fullest of God's blessings.

John 8:51

I tell you the truth, if anyone keeps my word, he will never see death.

A dear friend went home with Jesus recently. She had lived ninety-two years on this earth. There is a sense of loss for those who knew and loved her; yet going was her hope and her desire. The word "death" should not be used to describe her passing, for she was a Child of God. Death has no hold on her, no right to claim her. She merely left a broken, dying body in a broken, dying world...and she went home. The passing of a Christian who has lived a full life is not a reason to grieve. It is a time of reflection, a time to be grateful for the life that graced our own as long as God allowed. Our comfort lies in God's Word--in the promise that our lives, which truly began when we accepted Him, will never cease.

Jeremiah 31:34b

For I will forgive their wickedness and will remember their sins no more.

Do you wish you had a selective memory--the ability to remember only the things you wanted? Would you like to be able to blot out all the bad? I wish I could. There are many yesterdays I would remember no more, especially those when I allowed myself to wander out of God's will and into a scheme of Satan meant to destroy me. I remember those times… but God doesn't. God only remembers that I am His—a child that He will protect, provide for, and love forever. And guess what! That's what He remembers about you, too!

Hebrews 10:35,36 (The Message)

So don't throw it all away now. You were sure of yourselves then. It's still a sure thing! But you need to stick it out, staying with God's plan so you'll be there for the promised completion.

Satan loves to discourage Christians. He has many weapons he uses against us, trying to cause us to lose our determination, our zeal, and our joy in walking with God. He tries to instill doubt within us—doubt that we are being effective, that we are pleasing God, or that we are making a difference. If we are not careful, we will use criticism or difficulties as excuses for giving up. God's promises to us don't change. We can complete whatever course he sets us on, and we can complete it with victory. Life is not easy, and the road will never be smooth. There will be an end to all trouble, though, and through the grace of God we will arrive as conquerors.

Psalm 13:5-6

But I trust in your unfailing love; my heart rejoices in your salvation.
I will sing to the Lord, for He has been good to me.

I can't say that I have always trusted God completely. There have been times of weakness in the past, times when I looked for solutions I just could not find. I have racked my brain to come up with answers and doubted that any answers existed. I have spent many wasted hours worrying before I did what I should have done in the first place-- handed my problem over to God. Trusting God is easy if we remember all He has done for us, all the times He has rescued us, all the times He held us in His comforting, reassuring arms. His love is unfailing, unconditional, and unending. I pray that you worry about nothing today, but that you trust Him, singing and rejoicing because of His goodness and mercy toward you.

Psalm 10:4

In his pride the wicked does not seek Him; in all his thoughts there
is no room for God.

Our minds are wonderful, complicated parts of us. They are private, thinking secret thoughts that no one else can truly read or understand. While it is hard to say how much each mind is capable of holding, we can give importance to only a limited number of things. Satan works hard to fill our minds with earthly distractions—temporary plans, problems, and pleasures. This can weaken us and cause us to lose our joy and peace. Allowing Satan to fill our minds can also destroy us. What fills your thoughts? As you go about your day, what is your focus? I challenge you to crowd out the things that distract you and diminish your witness. Make room in your thoughts for God.

Isaiah 30:19b

How gracious He will be when you cry for help! As soon as He hears, He will answer you.

My granddaughter, like most two-year-olds, is an independent child. "I do it!" rings through the house dozens of times a day as she rejects attempts to help her do things she is determined to do on her own. Recently, to our shock, she added another dimension in her quest to conquer the world. When she failed at a task entirely too big for her, she bellowed for the first time, "I need help!" She had learned a lesson. Have we? God will let us try to do the impossible on our own if we insist. He won't force us to obey Him or walk the path that He has set before us. God is, however, always listening for our call. He longs to be gracious to us…remember? Don't ever think that you are strong enough, big enough, or smart enough to handle life on your own. Never think that God is too busy or too disgusted with you to help if you will call to Him. He loves you--completely, endlessly, and unconditionally. Need help? Tell Him.

Romans 8:38, 39

For I am convinced that neither death nor life, neither angels nor demons, neither the present nor the future, nor any powers, neither height nor depth, nor anything else in all creation, will ever be able to separate us from the love of God that is in Christ Jesus our Lord.

If my mind were completely stripped to the point I could remember only one thing about God, this would be my choice. God's love for me is permanent. Nothing can come between us. While we are in this world, many things can come against us. Diseases attack us, temptations deceive us, people betray us, and death takes those we love---but the love of our God, the Creator of the Universe, the King of Kings, is secure. God loves us even when we disobey and wander away from the path we know is right; He calls us back and welcomes us into His arms. Whatever problems, temptations, and trials you are facing today are temporary; they will pass. The love God has for you will endure forever. Hold your head high today, Child of God...Your Heavenly Father, Ruler of everything, adores you!

Romans 8:33,34

Who will bring any charge against those whom God has chosen? It is God who justifies. Who is he that condemns? Christ Jesus, who died—more than that, who was raised to life—is at the right hand of God and is also interceding for us.

In the final analysis, we have to answer to God only. We are not subject to the judgment of others. No matter what we have done, when we repent and come to Him--or come back to Him--He justifies us and cleanses us from all unrighteousness. Jesus Himself speaks to God on our behalf. I can imagine that He says, "Forgive her Father, for she is one of mine, made clean by the blood I shed for her." No one else has a right to bring charges against us, and Jesus won't. Just how awesome is that?

Luke 17:15-17

One of them (the ten lepers), when he saw he was healed, came back, praising God in a loud voice. He threw himself at Jesus' feet and thanked him—and he was a Samaritan. Jesus asked, "Were not all ten cleansed? Where are the other nine?"

Ten men who were suffering from leprosy stood by the road and cried out to Jesus. He had mercy on them and healed them all. Only one of them took the time to thank Him; the other nine just went on their way. What a lesson for us! Are we guilty? When we face trials and are filled with anxiety, what is our response when the trials are over and all is well? Too often, we accept the outcome and go on our way without acknowledging that God's hands moved in our behalf; He is the reason we are still standing, filled with peace and joy. Look around you. Consider where you are and where you would have been without Him. Don't be one of the nine; thank God for all He has done for you.

John 1:36,38a

When he (John) saw Jesus passing by, he said, "Look, the Lamb of God." When the two disciples heard him say this, they followed Jesus.

Turning around, Jesus saw them following and asked, "What do you want?"

Jesus' first recorded words in the Gospel of John were a question. I'm afraid far too many of us, in far too many instances, live day in and day out without actually knowing the answer. We are so tied up with the everydayness of our lives that we don't stop to analyze what is important. Life will be much fuller if use our energy to accomplish goals that draw us closer to God. If we use the wisdom He is willing to give us, we will strive to help those who need it, bring joy to those who know us, let others see God at work in our lives, and place Him first in everything. We do this not because we are required to. We do it because it is the only way to live happy, peaceful, and abundant lives. Answer this question for yourself today. What do you want?

Deuteronomy 10:14,15

To the Lord your God belong the heavens, even the highest heavens, the earth, and everything in it. Yet the Lord set His affection on your forefathers and loved them, and He chose you, their descendants, above all the nations as it is today.

Do you ever wonder why God bothers with us? We are so imperfect--so able to say and do hurtful things to each other, so likely to be wrapped up in ourselves, and so prone to act against His will. Everything that exists in the entire Universe belongs to Him, yet He values us most of all. He chose us to be His own. He set His affections upon us. He loves us. It isn't an accident that you are a Christian; He knocked on the door of your heart until you let Him in. It isn't an accident that you are reading this; He wanted to remind you of His love. He chose you. He chose me. He chose us to be His own, and He loves us more than anything. That is why He bothers.

Acts 4:10

Then know this, you and all the people of Israel: It is by the name of Jesus Christ of Nazareth, whom you crucified but whom God raised from the dead, that this man stands before you healed.

Could you begin count the times you have been in dire straits? Do you remember all the times you've thought, "I can't make it through this?" We all have had times when we wanted to give up...when we didn't think we could survive. But here we all are, in various stages of dealing with the onslaughts against us. In every case, God has picked us up, dusted us off, set us back on wobbly feet, and breathed new hope into our lives with His gentle reminder: "You can do all things through Christ, who strengthens you." The man in this account had been physically crippled, but regardless of what has been broken in our lives, our healing has come…and will continue to come…from the same source. We are survivors, standing today because of the name of Jesus Christ of Nazareth whom God raised from the dead.

2 Corinthians 5:17a

Therefore, if anyone is in Christ, he is a new creation.

God accepts us into His family just as we are. That doesn't mean, however, that He expects us to stay that way. Christ was willing to die on the cross to give us the greatest gift of all--a new life. It is tragic that so many Christians still trudge along in their old paths, content to accept the promise of eternal life He offers but doing little to help change their lives for the better here and now. God wants to do something through us, but first He has to be able to do something in us. I pray that we all may have a renewed revelation of the awesome gifts He has given us--the promise of eternal life with Him, the privilege of being called His children, and the honor of being His representatives here on earth. Don't attempt to take without giving. Give yourself completely to God, and let Him change your life forever.

1 Peter 1:23

For you have been born again, not of perishable seed, but of imperishable, through the living and enduring Word of God.

Some days it seems I tire very easily…probably because I try to do more than this body wants to do. It would be helpful if I could get a brand new body, one about 20 years old. But even if that were possible, that one would wear down, too. We are born in this world of perishable seed, and these bodies just will not last. We, however, will. We will live forever because our spirits have been born again of imperishable seed.

This is God's gift to us, made possible because Jesus was willing to give Himself to give us this new life. No matter how tired, worn down, or sick we are, there is still reason to rejoice because that is all temporary. Our spirits, the permanent part of us, will never die. We will live with Him forever. I feel energized just thinking about it.

Jonah 2:7

When my life was ebbing away, I remembered you, Lord, and my prayer rose to you, to your holy temple.

Jonah wasn't just having a bad day. Trapped in the belly of a big fish, he had some serious problems. Most of us have been in a place where we felt, as Jonah did, that our lives were slipping away. It might have been our health, our finances, our courage, our sense of well-being, or our relationships with other people or God Himself. Maybe we've been trapped in a place where we could see no escape. Even when we see no answer, there is one. Jonah prayed, and the answer to his dilemma came: God rescued him. No matter what may be wrong in your life, God can fix it. Let your prayers go up to Him and wait for Him to rescue you. Whether you are facing a major setback or just a bad day, God cares.

2 Chronicles 20:15

He said: "Listen, King Jehoshaphat and all who live in Judah and Jerusalem! This is what the Lord says to you: 'Do not be afraid or discouraged because of this vast army. For the battle is not yours, but God's.'"

If I had to give you advice with just two words, they might be "Let God." Why is this so hard? We think we are independent, trusting ourselves to solve whatever problems we encounter. Then when we face a crisis, we melt in fear. God wants us to lean on Him in everything. He willingly takes on our battles. He wants to step in and fight for His precious children…but He won't if we won't let Him. Trust Him with whatever problems you may be facing. Enjoy this beautiful day knowing that the God of all creation, your Savior and your King, is fighting your battle for you. And….He always wins!

Hebrews 4:12

For the Word of God is living and active. Sharper than any double-edged sword, it penetrates even to the dividing soul and spirit, joints and marrow; it judges the thoughts and attitudes of the heart.

There really isn't any good excuse for not knowing how God wants us to live. His will is not some mystical, mysterious, secret thing that only the wisest can figure out. God's Word is alive, working within us and telling us everything we need to know. It speaks to us where we are, about what concerns us. It convicts us of our wrong thoughts and attitudes while it encourages and builds us up. God's Word gives us strength and comfort; it gives us joy and healing for our bodies and our souls. It gives us hope; it gives us life. Don't let this day go by without soaking in some of His precious Word.

Jeremiah 23:24

"Can anyone hide in secret places so that I cannot see him?" declares the Lord. "Do I not fill heaven and earth?" declares the Lord.

If I could have hidden from God, there are times in the past when I would have. I didn't want Him to see that I was choosing to follow my own path instead of His. Having my whole life laid bare before His eyes, though, is actually a blessing. He saw my sin, but He forgave me. He also saw my hurt, my pain, my insecurity, my fears--my everything else that made me weak and stole my joy, and He held me in His arms and made me whole again. With all my failures, faults, and flaws, God loves me anyway—and He loves you, too. Be grateful that He knows you inside out. Be grateful that you can't hide from Him, for He is always watching to comfort, strengthen, and protect you--His precious child.

Matthew 16:22

Peter took Him (Jesus) aside and began to rebuke Him. "Never, Lord!" he said. "This shall never happen to you!"

In the verses before this, Jesus had been explaining to the disciples what was going to happen to Him regarding His death. Peter rebuked Him. He criticized Him sharply! What was Peter thinking? How could he have thought, even for a moment, that Jesus didn't know what He was talking about? Peter had his own plan: he wanted Jesus to set up an earthly kingdom then...not die on a Roman cross. It's easy for us to see that Peter's plan would have been a tragedy for us. God's plan, however unacceptable it was to Peter at the time, saved us from hopeless despair here on earth and eternal damnation. Often, our plans aren't best for us either, and our peace and joy in life depend upon our accepting that God knows what's best for us. If your plans aren't successful and your prayers aren't answered the way you want, rejoice anyway. Consider that God has a much better plan in store for you--one that is far better than you can imagine.

Isaiah 30:15a

This is what the Sovereign Lord, the Holy One of Israel says: "In repentance and rest is your salvation, in quietness and trust is your strength, but you would have none of it."

God created us with free will. We have the power to choose whether we will accept Jesus as our Savior or reject His gift of eternal salvation. We have the power to choose whether we will live in obedience or try to create our own plan for happiness. Many of God's external blessings still fall on those who reject Him, and on the outside, their lives may seem complete. But sunshine falls within only on those who claim Him, and only through Him can we have full, abundant lives. We always have a choice. My prayer for you today is that you will never miss a single blessing God wants to shower upon you because you would have none of it.

Colossians 1:13,14

For He has rescued us from the dominion of darkness and brought us into the kingdom of the Son He loves, in whom we have redemption, the forgiveness of sins.

If it weren't for God's great mercy, we would all be eternally trapped, doomed forever to be under Satan's absolute ownership. We are all guilty, and sinning gives supreme authority to the one who hates us all and has the sole goal of destroying us. But (sometimes I just love that word) because of God's amazing grace, He rescued us and brought us into the kingdom of Jesus Christ. Jesus willingly shed His precious, sinless blood, and paid the ransom to free us from our captivity. I am continually amazed that He cared enough to do this, but He did. Satan owns no part of us; the love of Jesus has set us free and brought us into His kingdom. Rejoice, Child of God; you have been forgiven and redeemed!

Psalm 103:13,14

As a father has compassion on his children, so the Lord has compassion on those who fear Him; for He knows how we are formed; He remembers that we are dust.

Many people who don't know God think of Him as some powerful entity, aloof and disinterested in man. They think He ignores us unless He decides to punish us for our failures. How wrong! God is aware of everything in our lives that brings us joy or pain…and He cares. He came to earth to take the punishment due us because of our sins; He tells us to cast our burdens on Him; He has shown us how to live lives of joy and peace. He understands our weaknesses, and He loves us even when we are wandering around on paths we have allowed Satan to set us on. Our compassionate, loving God is always watching, caring, and calling us to come home.

Psalm 46:10a

Be still, and know that I am God.

It would be impossible to single out my favorite Scripture, but this would be on the list. It is one that grounds me, one that brings me back when the problems of the world encroach upon my peace. When I get all caught up in the junk that invades the lives of all of us, I wish God would just grab me by the shoulders, shake me, and set me down. I need to hear Him say, "I love you, and I am in charge of every problem you will ever face. Nothing can separate you from my love!" He does not use force with us, though, and it is up to us to sit, drop to our knees, or fall on our faces… and just be still. My friends, our lives have joy, peace, and meaning only in His Presence and His will.

Isaiah 43:1b

Fear not, for I have redeemed you; I have summoned you by name; you are mine.

We all have titles of some sort. Each of us is somebody's mother, father, daughter, son, grandmother, grandfather, sister, brother, husband, wife, aunt, uncle, cousin, or friend. I treasure each of my relationships more than I could ever say. However, the title I value most is *Child of God*. I belong to the Creator of the Universe, the Almighty, the King of Kings. It's not because I was smart enough to seek Him; He summoned me. He redeemed me and called me out. He claimed me as His own. He loved me before He knit me together in my mother's womb, and He will never give me up...and you know what? He won't give you up, either! I hope you have a wonderful day reflecting on who...and whose...you are: a precious, redeemed, forgiven Child of God.

Genesis 15:6

Abram believed the Lord, and He credited it to him as righteousness.

Abram (Abraham) was not a perfect man, and yet he was righteous in God's eyes. This righteousness was not something he earned through great deeds. It was a gift, credited to him because he believed God. Think about this for a minute. This is wonderful news for all of us! We don't have to be sinless to be righteous in God's eyes. Christ took care of that once and for all, and it is His righteousness that covers us. All we have to do is believe God...believe that what He says is true and that what He says He will do, He will do. Spend time with Him today and thank Him for doing what you could have never done for yourself...for giving you the gift of right standing in His eyes.

Galatians 6:9

Let us not become weary in doing good, for at the proper time we will reap a harvest if we do not give up.

We like to see results. We tend to expect everything we do to produce results, and we'd like for them to be immediate. It's hard for us to get it through our thick skulls that God is never in a hurry. He has His own timetable, and it doesn't match ours. Everything we do for God accomplishes something...somewhere, sometime. He has a harvest time for us if we do not give up. We must keep on doing good by loving and helping others whether our actions seem to be having any effect or not. Don't give up. Don't be discouraged. Nothing we do for God goes unnoticed or unrewarded by the One who gives us life itself.

Acts 7:54,55,59,60

When they (the Jewish leaders) heard this, they were furious and gnashed their teeth at him. But Stephen, full of the Holy Spirit, looked up to heaven and saw the glory of God, and Jesus standing at the right hand of God...While they were stoning him, Stephen prayed, "Lord Jesus, receive my spirit." Then he fell on his knees and cried out, "Lord, do not hold this sin against them." When he had said this, he fell asleep.

Stephen was man filled with the Holy Spirit who did great wonders and performed miraculous signs among the people. The Jewish leaders wanted to silence Him, and so they brought false witnesses against him and stoned him to death. As a child, I thought this account had a bad ending. I wanted Jesus to zap the bad guys and save Stephen from the mob. But I see now that Stephen had a mighty role to play in the spread of the Gospel, and his death at the hands of the Jews was the key part. Stephen was willing. He was willing to be used however God wanted, willing to die rather than deny Jesus, and willing to forgive those who killed him. As Stephen fulfilled the role planned for Him from the beginning of time, he saw the glory of God and Heaven open. Whatever God asks us to do, however hard it may seem, God will give us the strength. If we are faithful, we can end our days here like Stephen, completing the task God has for us and seeing His glory as Heaven opens.

Ecclesiastes 5:19,20

Moreover, when God gives any man wealth and possessions, and enables him to enjoy them, to accept his lot and be happy in his work—this is a gift from God. He seldom reflects on the days of his life, because God keeps him occupied with gladness of heart.

Is your heart glad? It is so what God wants for your life, you know. He has promised us that He will provide for us, protect us, love us, and take us home to be with Him some day. Believing Him in these promises should bring us great joy! We can accept our lot, the things we cannot change, and endure without complaining. We can be happy in our daily tasks, whether we are at home or in the workplace. We won't spend our time reflecting on past sorrow or regret, and we won't lament over the "what-ifs" and all the things we don't have or can't do. God will be able to use us regardless of—or because of--our circumstances. And what's more, we can enjoy our lives as our Heavenly Father intended for us to do. May you have a wonderful day, totally occupied with gladness of heart!

Nahum 1:3b

His way is in the whirlwind and the storm, and clouds are the dust of His feet.

Life is not like a peaceful, glassy sea. It is filled with clouds, whirlwinds, and storms of all kinds. Even though we may wish for smooth sailing, it is through the rough spots of our lives that we learn to lean on God. How could we have faith if there were no clouds? How could we be certain that He would carry us through if there were no storms? One day we will see Him face to face in all His glory. Until then, draw near to Him and trust. I pray that you will feel His Presence in each whirlwind, storm, and cloud, for He will be there.

Jeremiah 31:3

The Lord appeared to us in the past saying, "I have loved you with an everlasting love; I have drawn you with loving-kindness."

How many times have you heard the expression, "Nothing lasts forever"? You've probably heard it more times than you can count, and in most cases, it is the truth. It is not true where our relationship with God is concerned. God loves us--period. He will love us forever--period. His love for us is tender and kind, and He is constantly working in our lives, drawing us into a closer relationship with Him. No matter how broken your life may seem at the moment, keep this thought at the forefront of your mind: God's love is yours forever. If you haven't told Him yet today, tell Him now. "Lord, I will love you forever, too!"

Judges 10:13-16

(God speaking) "But you have forsaken me and served other gods, so I will no longer save you. Go and cry out to the gods you have chosen. Let them save you when you are in trouble!"

But the Israelites said to the Lord, "We have sinned. Do with us whatever you think best, but please rescue us now." Then they got rid of the foreign gods among them and served the Lord. And He could bear Israel's misery no longer.

The Israelites had messed up. They had forsaken the Lord and served other gods. They deserved to have Him turn His back on them...and so do we. All of us have created new gods for ourselves at some point. We have let someone or something else take His place. What if we had to rely on these gods to save us? God told the Israelites to cry out to their other gods...and what did they do? They confessed their sins and repented, throwing themselves on God's mercy. What did God do? Our loving, merciful, compassionate Father could bear their misery no longer! It almost seems too easy, doesn't it? When they turned back to Him, He was there. He heard them, forgave them, and rescued them. I've been there, Brothers and Sisters, and it's true. God loves us so much that He can't bear our misery--even when we deserve it.

Mark 6:35-37

By this time it was late in the day, so His disciples came to Him. "This is a remote place," they said, "and it's already very late. Send the people away so they can go to the surrounding countryside and villages and buy themselves something to eat."

But He answered, "You give them something to eat."

The people in the crowd of five thousand were hungry. The disciples thought they should go away and feed themselves, but Jesus told the disciples to do it. We could wonder why Jesus didn't rain down fish like manna and feed them Himself, but He chose to work through His followers. Like the disciples in this case, we don't have what it takes to help others on our own. He can, however, equip us when we are willing. The gifts He has given us--including talent, time, money, and wisdom--are multiplied when we bring them to Jesus to use in the way that He wants. Never feel that you are not able. You can do anything that Jesus asks you to do, and He asks you to serve others He puts in your life.

1 Kings 19:11-13a

The Lord said, "Go out and stand on the mountain in the presence of the Lord, for the Lord is about to pass by." Then a great and powerful wind tore the mountains apart and shattered the rocks before the Lord, but the Lord was not in the wind. After the wind there was an earthquake, but the Lord was not in the earthquake. After the earthquake came a fire, but the Lord was not in the fire. And after the fire came a gentle whisper. When Elijah heard it, he pulled his cloak over his face and went out and stood at the mouth of the cave.

Do we sometimes miss out on what God is telling us because we are expecting something different? Maybe we expect Him to show Himself to us in mighty ways, to shake our world with undeniable signs. In this case, when Elijah needed answers for his nation and himself, his answer came in a whisper. God wants to guide us, too. He could speak to us in ways that show his all-powerful nature; but, more likely, He will speak through a gentle whisper, heard only by our hearts. God has the answers to any problem you have. Open your heart and listen.

James 1:2-4

Consider it pure joy, my brothers, whenever you face trials of many kinds, because you know that the testing of your faith develops perseverance. Perseverance must finish its work so that you may be mature and complete, not lacking anything.

Nearly every day we are faced with problems we didn't anticipate... problems with things, with people, even with ourselves. Something we need quits working; someone we care about disappoints or hurts us;

something new physically or emotionally challenges us or someone we love. God doesn't send all of these things our way, but each one can be an opportunity to grow. We can be angry and short-tempered with others, fight back, and feel sorry for ourselves; or we can step back and let God show us how to move on in peace. Persevering through all our problems and disappointments shows that we trust Him. It strengthens us and brings us closer to being all that He wants us to be. Look upon your trials as opportunities and rejoice, knowing that with God's help, you will conquer them all.

Amos 4:13

He who forms the mountains, creates the wind, and reveals His thoughts to man, He who turns dawn to darkness, and treads the high places of the earth—the Lord God Almighty is His name.

Most people who claim to believe in God accept the fact that He forms the mountains, creates the wind, turns dawn to darkness, and treads the high places of the earth. What about the fact that He is willing to reveal His thoughts to us? That is amazing! The Lord of the Universe will supernaturally show us truths beyond human vision or reason, things too wonderful for us to even imagine. He is not likely to surprise us with great revelation while we are busy with worldly tasks, though. He will reveal His thoughts to us when we are seeking Him with our whole hearts. As He promised Jeremiah, He will tell us great and unsearchable things we do not know. Spend time with your Creator, Lord, and King today and expect a revelation from His heart to yours.

Mark 6:31b

He (Jesus) said to them, "Come with me by yourselves to a quiet place and get some rest."

Oh, how I love this Scripture! It fills me with joy to know that Our Lord and King wants to spend time with me! It's not that He just allows me to be in His Presence--He yearns for my companionship! If we think about all He has done for each of us and the urgency of spreading His message, it would seem reasonable if He asked us to work constantly. However, to be productive for His Kingdom, we need the strength that is found only in spending time alone with Him. Don't ignore this marvelous invitation. Go with Him today to a quiet place and get some rest. Your King is waiting for you!

Isaiah 55:12

You will go out in joy and be led forth in peace; the mountains and hills will burst into song before you, and all the trees of the field will clap their hands.

Spring is a beautiful time in the Ozark foothills. The buds on the trees unfold into tiny green leaves, little flowers break through the warming earth, and the redbud--oh, the redbud! It is magnificent! There is a scientific explanation for spring, but to me, it is a special gift from God that brings me great joy. And isn't that just like Him? How many wondrous things does He do to give us pleasure just because He loves us? I hope that wherever you are today, you can enjoy the beauty of His creation. Praise God by clapping with the trees and bursting into song with the mountains and hills.

Luke 18:41

"What do you want me to do for you?"
"Lord, I want to see," he replied.

If Jesus asked you this question, what would you say? Speaking for myself, I think the blind man's answer might be mine also. "Lord, I want to see. I want to see your plan and purpose for my being. I want to see your hands at work in my life. I want to see your smiling face. I want to see your glory, Lord...I want to see you." There is nothing greater than His Presence in our lives. The pain we have in this world because of sickness, death, or betrayal is bearable because of Him. He is always there, yearning to wipe away our tears and hold us in His arms. Everything that gives us joy comes through His loving hands, and the closer we are to Him, the happier we become. He wants nothing more than to have a real relationship with us. Tell Him today. "Lord, I want to see...I want to see you."

Psalm 40:2

He lifted me out of the slimy pit, out of the mud and mire; He set my feet on a rock and gave me a firm place to stand.

God placed us on the Rock when we accepted Christ as our Savior. Unfortunately, stupidly, most of us have slipped, fallen, or jumped off at some point. We peeked over the side, saw what we thought were green pastures, and chose to leave our place of security. We soon discovered that what appeared to be a pleasant place was nothing more than quicksand intended to pull us under and destroy us. The good news-- the amazingly wonderful news--is that God will reach down and pull us up again...and again. Never think you've messed up so badly that God doesn't care anymore. He does. Never think you've gone too far to come back. You haven't. The safest place to be, though, is in the center. Don't wander to the edge. Don't even peek over the side. Stay in the safety and security of the center of God's will.

New Year's Day...Matthew 28:20b

And, lo, I am with you always--even unto the end of the world.

Jesus spoke these words at the end of the Great Commission. He had just instructed His followers to go throughout the world making disciples, baptizing them, and teaching them to obey God's commands. Above any other New Year's resolutions we may make, we should resolve to live our lives to please God and show His love by reaching out to others. We could not begin to count the blessings He has given us, and He has promised to continue watching over us and caring for us for all eternity. He will always be there, and He is everything we need. God's love is eternal. I wish you peace, health, love, and joy! Happy New Year!

Valentine's Day...Psalm 66:20

Praise be to God, who has not rejected my prayer or withheld His love from me!

I don't understand so many things about God. I don't understand how He has always been and always will be. I don't understand how He can be everywhere at the same time. I don't understand the power that created galaxies with a word. And I don't understand how or why He could care about me. Yet, I know without a doubt that all of these things are true. Praise His Name, for even if (when) we wander and rebel against His authority, He is always willing to welcome us back. He hears our prayers, and He loves us still. I pray that you feel surrounded by His love this Valentine's Day.

Easter...John 19:30

When He had received the drink, Jesus said, "It is finished." With that, He bowed His head and gave up His spirit.

On the night before and the day of Jesus' crucifixion, He suffered more than we even want to imagine. The soldiers cut his back open when they beat Him. They pierced His brow when they forced a crown of thorns upon His head. They pulled out His beard, spat on Him, slapped Him, and mocked Him. They drove nails into His hands and feet as they nailed Him on a cross to hang in public humiliation. Even worse was the wrath of God He faced for the disobedience of us all. He bore all the pain that should have been ours. This verse of Scripture contains some of the most meaningful words Jesus ever spoke. It signifies the completion of everything He came to earth to do. He came to teach us how to love, show us how to live, and give His perfect, sinless life to pay the price to save our broken, sinful souls. When He bowed His head and gave up His spirit, it was finished. My heart aches for the sins of mine He had to bear, but my heart rejoices that He loved me enough to do it. Celebrate today, for our Risen Savior has given us joy, hope, peace, and eternal life with Him!

Mothers' Day...Proverbs 23:25

May your father and mother be glad; may she who gave you birth rejoice!

We set aside today to honor mothers. Some of us still have our mothers on this earth, but many of us, like me, do not. I was blessed to have a Godly mother. She loved me unconditionally and was an inspiring example, my greatest defender, and my constant supporter. The best way I can honor her and her memory is to live my life the way she taught me--loving and obeying God. This is what would please her most. It is the highest calling for each of us and the only one that really matters. However you may celebrate this day, rededicate yourself to God, making your life a reason for your mother, children, family, and friends--for all who know you--to rejoice.

Fathers' Day...1 John 3:1a KJV

Behold, what manner of love the Father hath bestowed upon us, that we should be called the sons of God.

The third Sunday of every June, we celebrate Fathers' Day. It is a time for honoring and remembering the fathers who have touched our lives. Through the ages, good fathers have worked to provide for their families and devoted themselves to their protection. In some cases, they have been a guiding light, a supporting rock, and a safe shelter. All of the admirable traits that make a wonderful earthly father are those patterned after our Heavenly Father, who has taught us everything we know about loving and caring. I wish with all my heart that you were blessed with a wonderful earthly father, but if you weren't, know this: your Father in Heaven loves you more than any person ever could. As you remember your father today, be sure you remember your Father.

Fourth of July...2 Chronicles 7:14

If my people, who are called by my name, will humble themselves and pray and seek my face and turn from their wicked ways, then will I hear from heaven and will forgive their sin and will heal their land.

Our country is in trouble. Everywhere we look, our way of life is threatened by something. There are so many things we would like to see changed, and we feel powerless to do anything about them. It is easy to sit back and complain about mistakes others may have made and to fret because no one is coming up with real solutions. This is not the answer. God will forgive and heal our land if we who are called by His name do what we should be doing anyway: humble ourselves, pray, seek His face, and turn from our wicked ways. The urgency and importance of this can't be overstated. Our future and the future of our children and grandchildren depend on a strong, Christian country, and there is something we can do about it. Celebrate our country today. Enjoy the barbecue, ice cream, and fireworks...but don't forget to spend some time at God's throne praying for America.

Thanksgiving...Luke 10:38-42

As Jesus and his disciples were on their way, He came to a village where a woman named Martha opened her home to Him. She had a sister called Mary, who sat at the Lord's feet listening to what He said. But Martha was distracted by all the preparations that had to be made. She came to Him and asked, "Lord, don't you care that my sister has left me to do the work by myself? Tell her to help me!"

"Martha, Martha," the Lord answered, "you are worried and upset about many things, but only one thing is needed. Mary has chosen what is better, and it will not be taken from her."

In this account, Martha was working frantically, trying to prepare a meal for Jesus and who knows how many disciples. Mary was not helping her at all! Mary was just kicking back, sitting at the Lord's feet, listening to Him. I can imagine how Martha was fuming; I have done my fair share of that, too. But when Martha complained, Jesus told her that Mary was doing the important thing. As we approach Thanksgiving and Christmas, let's not be distracted by preparations for the things that are unimportant in the long run. Let's remember Jesus' words, "Only one thing is needed," and spend time at His feet, listening to Him.

Christmas...Psalm 51:16,17

You do not delight in sacrifice, or I would bring it; you do not take pleasure in burnt offerings. The sacrifices of God are a broken spirit; a broken and contrite heart, O God, you will not despise.

David, the author of this Psalm, knew there was nothing He could bring God that would atone for His sins. There is nothing we can bring Him, either...nothing we can do for Him that will please Him beyond this: He wants us to recognize our sins, repent, and follow the path He sets before us. When we are truly remorseful, we will feel the pain of a broken heart, broken because we have caused our Lord and Savior pain. Only when our spirits are broken will we be willing to let His Spirit take control of our lives. Then He can fill us with joy and use us to make a difference. This Christmas season is the perfect time to rid yourself of anything that stands between you and who you ought to be. Give God the only gift He wants.

Christmas...Luke 2:6,7

While they were there, the time came for the baby to be born, and she gave birth to her firstborn, a son. She wrapped him in cloths and placed him in a manger, because there was no room for them in the inn.

If God had chosen to do so, He could have forced the innkeeper to give Joseph and Mary a room. He could have required the finest accommodations, including all the homage due the King of the Universe.

He didn't, and Jesus was born in a manger because the innkeeper found no room. I imagine this had little or no impact on the life of the innkeeper. On the other hand, there are tragic results for the man who finds no room for Him in his heart today. We each have a choice. God will not force His Son on us any more than He forced Him on the innkeeper. One of the greatest gifts you can give yourself this Christmas is a serious examination of yourself. Are you making room for Him in your heart?

Christmas...Luke 1:38

"I am the Lord's servant," Mary answered. "May it be to me as you have said." Then the angel left her.

Mary really was amazing. According to tradition, she was between 13 and 15--a child in our culture. She had been told something that would change her life forever: she could have been cast aside and stoned for bearing this child! Who would believe that God was the father? Yet her response was quick and sure. "I am the Lord's servant; whatever He says, I will do." Far too many of us today fail to do what God wants when He has made His message very plain. We fail not because we may be cast aside and stoned. We fail to obey simply because we do not want to. It is not convenient. It doesn't fit the lifestyle we have chosen. What God asks of us is very little compared to what He asked of Mary. Can we follow the example of a little girl in Israel over 2000 years ago and simply obey Him?

Christmas...Isaiah 9:6a KJV

For unto us a child is born...

Today is the official day we celebrate the birth of our Savior. Preparations and plans have been in the making for weeks…even months. Billions of dollars have been spent on gifts. Millions of hours have been spent shopping, wrapping, traveling, and cooking. While all of that is overdone, I'm glad that people make a big deal out of Christmas. It is a big deal. Christmas is the season of hope renewed--hope in the little baby, Jesus Christ. Without Him, there is no hope. He was born for us. He lived for us. He died for us. And (drum roll) He is at the right hand of God making intercession for us. I pray that the significance of the baby's birth fills your heart with joy and hope and that you have the most wonderful Christmas ever. It is Jesus' birthday…but it's your day, too. That baby, born in a manger over 2000 years ago, has given you eternal life. Celebrate!

New Year's Eve…2 Corinthians 5:17

Therefore if any man be in Christ, he is a new creature: old things are passed away; behold, all things are become new.

Today we mark the end of another year. No doubt your life was a mixture of good and not so good--things you want to remember and things you'd prefer to forget. While we can choose to look back with sadness and regret, we should look forward to the future with hope. This hope is for one reason: Christ. He gave His life to give us new life…an abundant life of peace, joy, and confidence in the future. This new life began when we gave our hearts to Him, and it will last forever. As we enter the new year, let the failures of the past be in the past. Give your feelings of regret or sadness to God, and look forward each day to becoming more and more like our Savior. Tomorrow marks the beginning of a new year. I pray that it brings you renewed strength and health, renewed determination and dedication, renewed faith and hope.

LaVergne, TN USA
16 December 2010

209040LV00001B/132/P

9 781449 706418